PREFACE

In today's fast-paced world of software development, the demand for scalable, maintainable, and flexible architectures has never been higher. Microservices have taken centre stage, enabling companies to build systems that can grow and evolve as their needs change. Microservices offer a way to break down large, monolithic applications into smaller, more manageable services that can be deployed, updated, and scaled independently. However, with this flexibility comes complexity, managing communication between services, maintaining a clear separation of concerns, and ensuring that business logic stays clean and consistent across services can quickly become overwhelming.

This is where Clean Architecture steps in. Clean Architecture provides a powerful framework to address these challenges by enforcing a clear separation between the business logic (or domain), the application logic, and the infrastructure. By doing so, Clean Architecture allows microservices to remain modular and maintainable, ensuring that the core business rules are not tightly coupled to external frameworks, databases, or user interfaces.

As systems scale, so does the importance of maintainability. Clean Architecture supports this scalability by making each component of a system loosely coupled and easy to extend or modify. Whether you're adding new microservices, integrating new databases, or adjusting APIs, Clean Architecture's principles make these tasks more straightforward. It ensures that scalability is baked in, allowing the system to grow organically without introducing the technical debt that typically accompanies fast growth.

In this book, we will explore how Node.js and MongoDB fit perfectly into this landscape. Their lightweight, asynchronous, and flexible nature makes them ideal candidates for building microservice-based systems with Clean Architecture. Together, these technologies provide a solid foundation for developing high-performance, scalable applications.

Through practical examples, full code implementations, and detailed discussions, this book will walk you through the journey of implementing Clean Architecture in a Node.js ecosystem. From understanding the core concepts of Clean Architecture to building complex workflows with domain events and sagas, this book is designed to give you your first steps into Clean Architecture, providing a moderately comprehensive yet accessible introduction to the architecture.

In addition to the above, you'll learn about core concepts, design patterns, and advanced workflows like domain events and sagas. While this book offers a thorough introduction to the concepts, it represents the beginning of your journey into Clean Architecture, providing a solid foundation for future exploration and mastery.

JITHU MUSTHAKEEM

Author

CONTENTS

∞

CHAPTER 1
INTRODUCTION TO CLEAN ARCHITECTURE

1.1 Overview of Software Architecture

Software architecture is like the blueprint for building a skyscraper. Just as we wouldn't think of constructing a house without a proper plan, it's unwise to dive into building a complex app without a solid architecture in mind. Imagine this, would anyone want to live in a flat where the bathroom is right next to the kitchen, or where the doors don't fit their frames? Nah, right? In the same way, if we don't plan our software structure well, it can quickly turn into a nightmare, hard to maintain, even harder to scale and pretty much impossible to extend.

Software architecture defines how the components of our app interact, and how responsibilities are shared among them. The aim here is to build a system that can stand the test of time without turning into a "spaghetti code" mess. This is where the Clean Architecture can help.

1.2 Evolution of Architectural Styles

The journey through software architecture is a bit like a tour through time. Before we land on the elegance of Clean Architecture, let's make a few pit stops along the way to see how we got here.

Monolithic Architecture

Back in the day, apps were like a giant char kway teow; everything mixed together into one big serving. All the features, business logic, and data were tightly packed into one huge file or a few awkwardly connected files. It worked, but if one small thing broke, the whole dish would go wrong.

Example

```
// monolithic.js
const express = require('express');
```

```
const app = express();
const PORT = 3000;

let users = []; // User data is mixed with business logic

// Handle user registration
app.post('/register', (req, res) => {
  const user = { id: users.length + 1, name: req.body.name };
  users.push(user);
  res.json({ message: 'User registered', user });
});

// Handle retrieving user list
app.get('/users', (req, res) => {
  res.json(users);
});

// Handle user authentication (everything is mixed here)
app.post('/login', (req, res) => {
  const user = users.find((u) => u.name === req.body.name);
  if (user) {
    res.json({ message: 'Login successful' });
  } else {
    res.status(401).json({ message: 'User not found' });
  }
});

app.listen(PORT, () => console.log(`Server running on port ${PORT}`));
```

What's happening? Everything is crammed into one place; data, business logic, and routes. If we want to change the user authentication flow, we risk breaking other parts of the app.

Layered (N-tier) Architecture:

Then came layered architecture, and suddenly, things got a bit more organised. We separated concerns into neat layers: UI Layer, Business Logic Layer, and Data Access Layer. But sometimes, these layers got too chummy and tightly coupled, making it tough to change things without breaking something else.

Example

Data Access Layer (data-access.js)

```
// data-access.js

const users = [];

function saveUser(user) {
  users.push(user);
}

function getUsers() {
  return users;
}

function findUserByName(name) {
  return users.find((user) => user.name === name);
}

module.exports = { saveUser, getUsers, findUserByName };
```

Business Logic Layer (user-service.js)

```
// user-service.js

const { saveUser, findUserByName } = require('./data-access');

function registerUser(name) {
  const user = { id: Date.now(), name };
  saveUser(user);
  return user;
```

```
}

function authenticateUser(name) {
  const user = findUserByName(name);
  return user ? 'Login successful' : 'User not found';
}

module.exports = { registerUser, authenticateUser };
```

UI Layer (routes.js)

```
// routes.js (UI Layer)

const express = require('express');
const app = express();
const { registerUser, authenticateUser } = require('./user-service');
const PORT = 3000;

app.post('/register', (req, res) => {
  const user = registerUser(req.body.name);
  res.json({ message: 'User registered', user });
});

app.post('/login', (req, res) => {
  const message = authenticateUser(req.body.name);
  res.json({ message });
});

app.listen(PORT, () => console.log(`Server running on port ${PORT}`));
```

What's happening? We've separated data handling, business logic, and routes into different files. This makes things more modular, but if the data access method changes, it might still affect the business logic.

Microservices

Now, we level up to the microservices, like breaking up our char kway teow into separate plates for each ingredient. Each service became a self-contained unit that could be deployed independently. They worked well, but needed some coordination to come together as a full meal.

Example

User Service (user-service.js)

```
// user-service.js

const express = require('express');
const app = express();
const PORT = 3001;
let users = [];

app.post('/register', (req, res) => {
  const user = { id: Date.now(), name: req.body.name };
  users.push(user);
  res.json({ message: 'User registered', user });
});

app.listen(PORT, () => console.log(`User Service running on port ${PORT}`));
```

Product Service (product-service.js)

```
// product-service.js

const express = require('express');
const app = express();
const PORT = 3002;
let products = [];

app.post('/add-product', (req, res) => {
  const product = { id: Date.now(), name: req.body.name };
  products.push(product);
  res.json({ message: 'Product added', product });
```

```
});

app.listen(PORT, () => console.log(`Product Service running on port ${PORT}`));
```

API Gateway (api-gateway.js)

```
// api-gateway.js

const express = require('express');
const axios = require('axios');
const app = express();
const PORT = 3000;


app.use(express.json());

app.post('/register', async (req, res) => {
  const response = await axios.post('http://localhost:3001/register', req.body);
  res.json(response.data);
});

app.post('/add-product', async (req, res) => {
  const response = await axios.post('http://localhost:3002/add-product', req.body);
  res.json(response.data);
});

app.listen(PORT, () => console.log(`API Gateway running on port ${PORT}`));
```

What's happening? Here, user-service and product-service are independent services, each with its own responsibilities. The api-gateway coordinates between them. They can be scaled or updated independently, but setting up communication between services adds complexity.

Clean Architecture

And now, Clean Architecture enters the chat! It builds on the good parts from older styles but takes it a step further, offering a structure that keeps layers independent, loose, and easy to test, extend, and maintain.

Example

Entities (User.js)

```
// entities/User.js

class User {
  constructor(id, name) {
    this.id = id;
    this.name = name;
  }
}

module.exports = User;
```

Use Case (registerUser.js):

```
// use-cases/registerUser.js

const User = require('../entities/User');

function registerUser(userRepository, name) {
  const user = new User(Date.now(), name);
  userRepository.save(user);
  return user;
}

module.exports = registerUser;
```

Interface Adapter (UserRepository.js)

```
// interface-adapters/UserRepository.js

let users = [];
```

```
function save(user) {
  users.push(user);
}

function findByName(name) {
  return users.find((user) => user.name === name);
}

module.exports = { save, findByName };
```

Framework (server.js)

```
// frameworks/server.js

const express = require('express');
const app = express();
const registerUser = require('../use-cases/registerUser');
const userRepository = require('../interface-adapters/UserRepository');
const PORT = 3000;

app.use(express.json());

app.post('/register', (req, res) => {
  const user = registerUser(userRepository, req.body.name);
  res.json({ message: 'User registered', user });
});

app.listen(PORT, () => console.log(`Server running on port ${PORT}`));
```

What's happening? Clean Architecture separates each part into distinct layers. The entities are pure JavaScript classes that represent our core logic. Use cases handle specific operations. Interface adapters translate between external inputs and the core logic. Frameworks like Express only handle routing and external interactions. If you want to change from a REST API to GraphQL or switch databases, it doesn't affect your core logic.

1.3 What is Clean Architecture?

Clean Architecture is like that methodical, disciplined kung fu master, created by Robert C. Martin (Uncle Bob). It emphasises keeping our core logic clean and free from the entanglements of external frameworks like Express or databases like MongoDB.

Here's a fun analogy:

Imagine we're building a robot (because, why not?). The core logic, the bits that make the robot think and move is like our business logic. The robot's arms, legs, sensors, and speakers are like interface adapters that help it interact with the world. Now, if we want to upgrade the robot's arms without messing with its brain, Clean Architecture is what allows us to do that! We can change or add external parts (like a new UI or database) without breaking the robot's core logic.

The Core Principles of Clean Architecture

1. **Separation of Concerns**: Keep different responsibilities in different parts of the code. This means keeping business logic separate from things like databases or web frameworks.

2. **The Dependency Rule**: Dependencies should always point inward toward our core business logic. The outside layers (databases, frameworks, UI) shouldn't know what's happening inside.

3. **Testability**: Make testing a breeze. By keeping things separate, we can test each piece without it affecting others, catching bugs quickly.

4. **Maintainability and Extensibility**: With a clean structure, we can add new features and fix bugs without creating a domino effect of errors throughout the codebase.

1.4 Principles of Clean Architecture

The Dependency Rule

At the heart of Clean Architecture lies the "Dependency Rule." It's simple yet super powerful: **Dependencies always point inward.** That means our core business logic shouldn't know or care about details like databases or how the user interface looks. This makes it super easy to swap out or upgrade external systems without breaking our business logic.

Key Layers in Clean Architecture

Entities (Core Business Rules)

The heart and soul of our application. Think of these as the main characters in our story, they represent the business objects and their relationships. They have no idea about databases, web servers, or any of that external stuff.

Use Cases (Application Business Rules)

This is where the plot thickens. Use cases define what our app can do. They control how data flows between entities and the outside world.

Interface Adapters (Controllers, Gateways)

The middleman of our story. These convert external inputs (like HTTP requests) into something our core logic understands.

Frameworks & Drivers (UI, DB, Web Frameworks)

These are like the sidekicks, Express.js, MongoDB, or other frameworks that our system uses to interact with the outside world.

1.5 Why Choose Clean Architecture for Node.js and MongoDB?

Node.js and MongoDB, a power couple for modern web apps! Node.js gives us that smooth, non-blocking performance, while MongoDB's NoSQL, document-based structure is perfect for dynamic and scalable applications. But without proper architecture, we can end up with a jungle of callbacks, async nightmares, and code that's messier than an unkempt hawker stall.

Clean Architecture is like our secret weapon when working with Node.js because it helps us:

- Separate the async logic from external stuff like databases and request handling.

- Keep our code modular and easy to test.

- Make it painless to swap databases (maybe moving from MongoDB to PostgreSQL) or switch frameworks (from Express to Fastify) without having to rewrite our core logic.

Here's a simple diagram to illustrate how Clean Architecture pieces fit together:

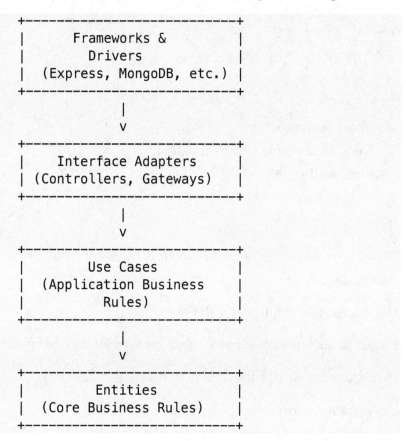

```
+----------------------------+
|       Frameworks &         |
|         Drivers            |
|   (Express, MongoDB, etc.) |
+----------------------------+
              |
              v
+----------------------------+
|     Interface Adapters     |
|   (Controllers, Gateways)  |
+----------------------------+
              |
              v
+----------------------------+
|        Use Cases           |
|   (Application Business     |
|         Rules)             |
+----------------------------+
              |
              v
+----------------------------+
|         Entities           |
|    (Core Business Rules)   |
+----------------------------+
```

1.6 Clean Architecture Layers: A Deeper Dive

Entities: The Heartbeat of Your Application

Entities are like the heartbeat of our application, they define the core data and rules.

Let's write a simple **Entity** for a User in Node.js:

```
class User {
  constructor(id, name, email) {
    this.id = id;
    this.name = name;
    this.email = email;
```

```
  }

  changeEmail(newEmail) {
    if (!this.validateEmail(newEmail)) {
      throw new Error('Invalid email format');
    }
    this.email = newEmail;
  }

  validateEmail(email) {
    // Simulate a simple email validation
    return email.includes('@');
  }
}
```

Notice how this entity doesn't know a thing about databases or HTTP requests. It's pure business logic!

Use Cases: The Application Brain

Use Cases define what happens when the user interacts with our system.

Here's an example of a use case to update a user's email:

```
class UpdateUserEmail {
  constructor(userRepository) {
    this.userRepository = userRepository;
  }

  execute(userId, newEmail) {
    const user = this.userRepository.findById(userId);
    user.changeEmail(newEmail);
    this.userRepository.save(user);
  }
}
```

The **use case** doesn't care if the data comes from MongoDB or somewhere else. It just orchestrates the business logic.

Interface Adapters: The Middleman

Interface Adapters make sure our use cases and entities can talk to the outside world without getting messy.

For example, here's a **Controller** using the UpdateUserEmail use case:

```
const express = require('express');

const app = express();


app.put('/users/:id/email', (req, res) => {
  const { id } = req.params;
  const { email } = req.body;


  try {
    updateUserEmail.execute(id, email); // Executes the use case
    res.status(200).send('Email updated successfully');
  } catch (err) {
    res.status(400).send(err.message);
  }
});
```

The controller acts as a translator, taking an HTTP request, passing it to our use case, and then sending back a response.

Summary

Clean Architecture is all about keeping our core business logic (Entities and Use Cases) separate from the outside world like frameworks and databases. By sticking to the Dependency Rule, we make sure that our business rules stay untangled from external influences. This makes our code base more maintainable, flexible, and testable.

CHAPTER 2
GETTING STARTED WITH NODE.JS AND MONGODB

We think of this chapter as the groundwork before building our sleek, well-oiled, and scalable application with Node.js and MongoDB. Imagine we're about to build our dream condo, before we get into the fancy designs, we need to ensure the foundations are solid. Instead of concrete and steel beams, we're using JavaScript and NoSQL databases. Ready to get your hands dirty with code? Let's dive in!

2.1 Introduction to Node.js

Node.js is like the *Swiss Army knife* for backend developers. Fast, versatile, and it's got a ton of tools (libraries) you can just plug and play. But why is it so shiok for us to use?

Non-blocking I/O Model

This is the power-up that makes Node.js stand out! Traditional servers are like our kiasu friends, if you ask them to get bubble tea, they'll queue until it's ready before doing anything else. But Node.js? Wah, it's like the busy uncle at the hawker centre, multitasking like nobody's business! It's non-blocking, meaning it doesn't just wait around, it handles multiple requests at the same time.

Think of it like this: a fast-food chef, grilling the patties while assembling burgers and taking orders, all at once. So Node.js is perfect for real-time apps, where we can't afford to wait!

Event-driven Architecture

At the core of Node.js is its event-driven approach. Events trigger actions, like how we get up when the MRT door chime rings. Node.js doesn't waste time waiting; it just moves on to the next task, which makes it super-efficient when dealing with I/O-heavy stuff like hundreds of HTTP requests.

Example of Non-blocking Code in Node.js

Here's a simple example to see Node.js in action:

```
const fs = require('fs');

console.log('Start reading file...');

fs.readFile('example.txt', 'utf8', (err, data) => {
  if (err) {
    console.error('Error reading file', err);
    return;
  }
  console.log('File content:', data);
});

console.log('File reading initiated!');
```

Output:

Start reading file...

File reading initiated!

File content: Hello, Node.js!

Notice how Node.js doesn't wait for the file to finish reading, it moves on and comes back when it's ready. Super efficient, right?

2.2 Introduction to MongoDB

Now let's talk about MongoDB. This is the database that's super chill, kind of like that friend who doesn't mind if your room's a mess, as long as you can find your things. Unlike SQL databases that demand everything to be neatly folded and labeled, MongoDB is okay with things being a little more freeform.

Key Concepts in MongoDB

- **Document-based**: MongoDB uses **documents** (which look a lot like JSON objects) to store data, so it's easy to work with complex data structures.

15

- **Collections**: Documents are stored in collections (similar to tables in SQL, but without the rigid structure).

- **Dynamic Schema**: You can add different fields to each document within a collection, like having a pizza where each slice has different toppings!

It's perfect for agile development, letting us change things on the fly, without needing to make rigid schema changes.

Example of a MongoDB Document

```
{
 "_id": "60e73a056cf1f540b5a61d4a",
 "name": "John Doe",
 "email": "john.doe@example.com",
 "age": 30,
 "address": {
  "street": "123 Elm Street",
  "city": "Springfield"
 }
}
```

You see? It's just a JSON object, easy-peasy.

Key MongoDB Operations

Here's a few must-know operations that will make you feel like a MongoDB pro:

1. **Inserting a Document**:

```
db.users.insertOne({
 name: "John Doe",
 email: "john.doe@example.com",
 age: 30
});
```

2. **Finding a Document**:

```
db.users.find({ name: "John Doe" });
```

3. Updating a Document:

```
db.users.updateOne({ name: "John Doe" }, { $set: { age: 31 } });
```

4. Deleting a Document:

```
db.users.deleteOne({ name: "John Doe" });
```

It's like sending orders to the kitchen, quick, clear, and no need to worry about strict table manners.

2.3 Setting Up the Development Environment

Ready to roll up our sleeves? It's time to set up our playground for Node.js and MongoDB. Let's make sure everything is ready before we start coding like pros!

Step 1: Installing Node.js

Head over to Node.js and grab the latest version. After installing, let's make sure Node.js and npm (Node Package Manager) are all set up:

node -v

npm -v

See some version numbers? Good, it means we're all set to start our coding adventure!

Step 2: Installing MongoDB

We've got two choices here:

1. Install MongoDB on your machine, follow the instructions from MongoDB's official site.

2. Use MongoDB Atlas, a cloud-hosted version that's super easy to start with (and got free tiers).

Once it's set up, make sure MongoDB is running by typing this in the terminal:

mongod

Boom! Your local MongoDB server is up and running.

Step 3: Creating Your First Node.js Project

Time to set up our project using **npm** (Node's package manager):

mkdir clean-architecture-node-mongo

cd clean-architecture-node-mongo

npm init -y

This generates a package.json file, which is like the control centre of your Node.js project, tracking all your dependencies (the tools and libraries you use).

Step 4: Installing Necessary Packages

Let's add the core packages that'll get us going:

npm install express mongoose dotenv

- **Express**: A minimal framework for building web apps in Node.js.
- **Mongoose**: An ODM (Object Data Mapper) that makes using MongoDB even simpler.
- **dotenv**: Lets us handle environment variables neatly.

Step 5: Setting Up ESLint and Prettier

For clean and consistent code, let's use **ESLint** for checking our code and **Prettier** for formatting:

npm install eslint prettier eslint-config-prettier eslint-plugin-prettier --save-dev

Initialize ESLint:

npx eslint --init

Choose these options:

1. To check syntax, find problems, and enforce code style

2. CommonJS (require/exports)

3. None of these (No framework)

4. No (Not using TypeScript)

5. Node

6. Use a popular style guide

7. Airbnb

8. JSON (Config file format)

Now add Prettier's config to your package.json:

```
"prettier": {
 "semi": false,
 "singleQuote": true
}
```

2.4 Creating Our First Node.js Project

Let's build a basic app that talks to MongoDB using Express.

Step 1: Setting Up Environment Variables

Create a .env file in the project's root directory and add this:

PORT=3000

MONGO_URI=mongodb://localhost:27017/cleanArchitecture

This way, sensitive details like our MongoDB connection string are safely stored.

Step 2: Basic Express Server

Let's create our first server in server.js:

```
require('dotenv').config();

const express = require('express');
const mongoose = require('mongoose');

const app = express();
app.use(express.json());

mongoose.connect(process.env.MONGO_URI, { useNewUrlParser: true,
useUnifiedTopology: true })
  .then(() => console.log('MongoDB connected!'))
  .catch(err => console.error('MongoDB connection error:', err));
```

```
app.get('/', (req, res) => {
  res.send('Hello, Clean Architecture!');
});

const port = process.env.PORT || 3000;
app.listen(port, () => {
  console.log(`Server running on port ${port}`);
});
```

Run it with:

node server.js

Head to http://localhost:3000 in your browser and you'll see "Hello, Clean Architecture!" It's like our version of "Hello World!"

Step 3: Adding a Mongoose Model

Let's define a **User** model in models/User.js:

```
const mongoose = require('mongoose');

const userSchema = new mongoose.Schema({
  name: { type: String, required: true },
  email: { type: String, required: true, unique: true },
  age: Number,
});

const User = mongoose.model('User', userSchema);

module.exports = User;
```

Step 4: Creating Routes for Users

Set up CRUD routes for users in routes/userRoutes.js:

```
const express = require('express');
const router = express.Router();
const User = require('../models/User');
```

```
router.get('/', async (req, res) => {
  const users = await User.find();
  res.json(users);
});

router.post('/', async (req, res) => {
  const { name, email, age } = req.body;
  const user = new User({ name, email, age });
  await user.save();
  res.status(201).json(user);
});

module.exports = router;
```

Step 5: Integrating Routes in Server

Finally, plug in the routes in server.js:

```
const userRoutes = require('./routes/userRoutes');
app.use('/users', userRoutes);
```

Now you can create, read, and manage users via the /users endpoint!

Summary

We've set up the groundwork for our Node.js and MongoDB application. Installed Node.js and MongoDB, and set up a basic Express server. Added crucial tools like Mongoose and dotenv for database connections and configuration. Created our first data model and set up routes for user management.

CHAPTER 3
APPLYING CLEAN ARCHITECTURE TO NODE.JS AND MONGODB

We've set up our basics with Node.js and MongoDB, but now, let's kick it up a notch. It's time to give our project some structure, think of it like upgrading from a simple coffee shop to a fancy artisanal café. In this chapter, we'll apply Clean Architecture principles to our project, transforming our basic Express server into a scalable, maintainable system. Picture our previous code as a humble HDB flat; now, we're turning it into a smart condo, no more chaos, just a streamlined, efficient setup.

We'll get cozy with how Clean Architecture fits into our Node.js and MongoDB application and give our code a makeover to match this approach.

3.1 Revisiting the Clean Architecture Structure

Before we jump straight into the code, let's do a quick refresh on the structure of Clean Architecture. The main idea here is to keep our business logic as pure as a freshly brewed coffee, untouched by external systems like databases, frameworks, or user interfaces. Our system is split into layers, each with a special role, so no one crosses into each other's turf.

Here's the lowdown on the layers:

Entities: Think of these as the core brain of our app, the solid "lah" of the business logic. In Node.js, they're usually represented as classes or objects that define the essential rules.

Use Cases: These fellas handle the specific business rules for the app, coordinating interactions between entities and outside components. They're like the kaypoh uncles making sure everything's in order.

Interface Adapters: These are the go-betweens, translating what the use cases need into something the outside world understands. For example, a web controller would convert HTTP requests into friendly instructions for our use cases.

Frameworks & Drivers: This is where all the external stuff lives, our web frameworks (Express), databases (MongoDB), and UI (like React, if you're feeling fancy). The beauty here is that they can be swapped out without messing up our core logic.

Clean Architecture Diagram

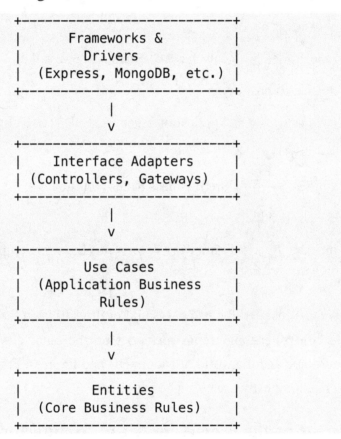

```
+-------------------------------+
|        Frameworks &           |
|          Drivers              |
|    (Express, MongoDB, etc.)   |
+-------------------------------+
                |
                v
+-------------------------------+
|      Interface Adapters       |
|   (Controllers, Gateways)     |
+-------------------------------+
                |
                v
+-------------------------------+
|         Use Cases             |
|   (Application Business       |
|          Rules)               |
+-------------------------------+
                |
                v
+-------------------------------+
|          Entities             |
|    (Core Business Rules)      |
+-------------------------------+
```

Our goal in this chapter is to refactor our project using this Clean Architecture, making sure each layer is well-defined, modular, and testable, like a good bowl of laksa, each part is distinct but blends beautifully together.

3.2 Setting Up the Directory Structure

To follow Clean Architecture properly, we need to tidy up our project directory. Here's a suggested layout for our Node.js app:

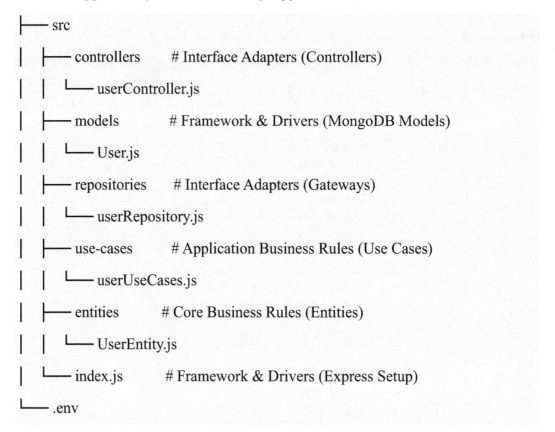

```
├── src
│   ├── controllers      # Interface Adapters (Controllers)
│   │   └── userController.js
│   ├── models           # Framework & Drivers (MongoDB Models)
│   │   └── User.js
│   ├── repositories     # Interface Adapters (Gateways)
│   │   └── userRepository.js
│   ├── use-cases        # Application Business Rules (Use Cases)
│   │   └── userUseCases.js
│   ├── entities         # Core Business Rules (Entities)
│   │   └── UserEntity.js
│   └── index.js         # Framework & Drivers (Express Setup)
└── .env
```

See how we've separated the **use cases** and **entities** to keep them at the heart of the app, while **controllers** and **repositories** sit on the outside, acting as middlemen between our logic and the world of MongoDB and Express. Everything in its proper place, just like our neatly organised coffee shop!

3.3 Refactoring the Project for Clean Architecture

Step 1: Creating the Entities (Core Business Logic)

Entities in Clean Architecture represent the core rules and concepts of the business. Let's start with defining a **UserEntity**. It'll handle user-related logic like verifying email addresses, no database or HTTP nonsense here, just pure logic.

Create src/entities/UserEntity.js

```javascript
// UserEntity.js
class UserEntity {
  constructor({ id, name, email, age }) {
    this.id = id;
    this.name = name;
    this.email = email;
    this.age = age;
  }

  changeEmail(newEmail) {
    if (!this.validateEmail(newEmail)) {
      throw new Error('Invalid email format');
    }
    this.email = newEmail;
  }

  validateEmail(email) {
    const emailRegex = /^[^\s@]+@[^\s@]+\.[^\s@]+$/;
    return emailRegex.test(email);
  }
}

module.exports = UserEntity;
```

Our UserEntity focuses only on user-specific logic, like changing an email and making sure it's valid. It's blissfully unaware of databases, HTTP requests, or other frameworks, like a carefree uncle playing chess at the kopitiam (coffee shop).

Step 2: Use Cases (Application Logic)

The **Use Case** layer handles application-specific rules, like coordinating what happens when we create or update a user. It's the one pulling the strings behind the scenes.

Create src/use-cases/userUseCases.js

```javascript
// userUseCases.js

const UserEntity = require('../entities/UserEntity');

class UserUseCases {
  constructor(userRepository) {
    this.userRepository = userRepository;
  }

  async createUser(userData) {
    const user = new UserEntity(userData);
    return this.userRepository.save(user);
  }

  async updateUserEmail(userId, newEmail) {
    const user = await this.userRepository.findById(userId);
    if (!user) {
      throw new Error('User not found');
    }
    user.changeEmail(newEmail);
    return this.userRepository.save(user);
  }

  async getAllUsers() {
    return this.userRepository.findAll();
  }
}

module.exports = UserUseCases;
```

The use cases handle the flow of creating users, updating their emails, and fetching them. Notice how it delegates data storage to the **repository**, keeping itself as database-agnostic as possible, like a hawker who only cares about making the best char kway teow, no matter where the ingredients come from.

Step 3: Repository Layer (Interface Adapter)

Repositories act as adapters between our core logic and the database, keeping things smooth and abstracted. It's like an expressway connecting two busy parts of town.

Create src/repositories/userRepository.js

```
// userRepository.js
const UserModel = require('../models/User');

class UserRepository {
 async findById(id) {
  const user = await UserModel.findById(id);
  if (!user) return null;
  return user.toObject();
 }

 async save(userEntity) {
  const userRecord = new UserModel(userEntity);
  await userRecord.save();
  return userRecord.toObject();
 }

 async findAll() {
  const users = await UserModel.find();
  return users.map(user => user.toObject());
 }
}

module.exports = UserRepository;
```

The repository takes care of fetching and saving users to MongoDB. This way, if we ever decide to switch from MongoDB to, say, PostgreSQL, our core logic remains untouched, like a stall that changes suppliers without customers noticing.

Step 4: MongoDB Model (Framework & Drivers)

MongoDB models live in the **Framework & Drivers** layer. Here, we define how data is stored in MongoDB.

Create src/models/User.js

```
// User.js

const mongoose = require('mongoose');


const userSchema = new mongoose.Schema({
  name: { type: String, required: true },
  email: { type: String, required: true, unique: true },
  age: { type: Number }
});


const UserModel = mongoose.model('User', userSchema);


module.exports = UserModel;
```

Our UserModel defines the structure for storing users in MongoDB. However, it's tucked behind the repository so our business logic remains blissfully unaware of how the data is actually stored.

Step 5: Controllers (Interface Adapters)

Controllers handle HTTP requests and pass the relevant data to the use cases. In Clean Architecture, they should stay slim and trim, like a kopi O kosong.

Create src/controllers/userController.js

```
// userController.js

const UserUseCases = require('../use-cases/userUseCases');
const UserRepository = require('../repositories/userRepository');
```

```javascript
const userRepository = new UserRepository();
const userUseCases = new UserUseCases(userRepository);
const userController = {
  createUser: async (req, res) => {
    try {
      const user = await userUseCases.createUser(req.body);
      res.status(201).json(user);
    } catch (error) {
      res.status(400).json({ message: error.message });
    }
  },

  updateUserEmail: async (req, res) => {
    const { id } = req.params;
    const { email } = req.body;

    try {

const updatedUser = await userUseCases.updateUserEmail(id, email);
      res.status(200).json(updatedUser);
    } catch (error) {
      res.status(400).json({ message: error.message });
    }
  },

  getAllUsers: async (req, res) => {
    const users = await userUseCases.getAllUsers();
    res.status(200).json(users);
  }
};

module.exports = userController;
```

Our controller takes care of transforming HTTP requests into instructions for the use cases. It's all about keeping things lean and efficient, like a true blue Singaporean queueing for the best hawker food.

Step 6: Setting Up Routes and Express (Framework & Drivers)

Time to wire everything up and get our app running.

Modify src/index.js

```
// index.js

require('dotenv').config();
const express = require('express');
const mongoose = require('mongoose');
const userController = require('./controllers/userController');

const app = express();
app.use(express.json());

mongoose.connect(process.env.MONGO_URI, { useNewUrlParser: true,
useUnifiedTopology: true })
  .then(() => console.log('MongoDB connected'))
  .catch((err) => console.error('MongoDB connection error:', err));

app.post('/users', userController.createUser);
app.put('/users/:id/email', userController.updateUserEmail);
app.get('/users', userController.getAllUsers);

const port = process.env.PORT || 3000;
app.listen(port, () => {
  console.log(`Server running on port ${port}`);
});
```

3.4 Testing Our Clean Architecture

Time to test if everything works like it should! Let's fire up our server and try a few requests.

1. **Start the server**:

```
node src/index.js
```

2. **Create a user**:

```
curl -X POST http://localhost:3000/users \
  -H "Content-Type: application/json" \
  -d '{"name": "John Doe", "email": "john@example.com", "age": 30}'
```

3. **Get all users**:

```
curl http://localhost:3000/users
```

4. **Update user email**:

```
curl -X PUT http://localhost:3000/users/{user_id}/email \
  -H "Content-Type: application/json" \
  -d '{"email": "new.email@example.com"}'
```

3.5 Why This Matters

With Clean Architecture, we've shaped our app to be:

- **Testable**: Each layer is independent, so we can test use cases without touching databases or HTTP stuff.

- **Scalable**: Adding new features becomes easy, just like adding a new stall to a hawker centre.

- **Maintainable**: By keeping things separate, it's easier to see what each part does, reducing bugs and making life easier for our future selves.

Summary

We've taken our Node.js and MongoDB app from a simple, flat setup to a clean, scalable, and maintainable architecture. Now, our code is structured in a way that makes it easy to expand and modify without breaking other parts. We're all set for the next chapter, where we'll dive into **testing strategies** to ensure our architecture holds up under pressure. Exciting times ahead!

CHAPTER 4
TESTING THE CLEAN ARCHITECTURE IN NODE.JS

Hey lah, welcome to Chapter 4! This is where things start to heat up. By now, we've built a nice and clean architecture for our Node.js app, structured just right with MongoDB. But come on, we all know an app that hasn't been tested is like a coffee shop without coffee, it just doesn't cut it. If we leave it unchecked, one small bug could collapse the whole thing like a house of cards. That's why in this chapter, we're diving into testing, the superhero that saves our code from chaos. Think of it like setting up smart alarms all over your fancy automated home, if something goes wrong, you'll be the first to know!

Shiok? Ready to take our app to the next level? Let's dive into testing and learn how to keep our Clean Architecture rock-solid.

4.1 Why Testing Matters in Clean Architecture

In Clean Architecture, each layer has its own special job, making it way easier to test parts of the system one by one. Testing isn't just a "nice to have," it's a must if we want to keep our code maintainable and bug-free. Here's what we're going to do:

Unit Testing: Test individual components, like entities and use cases, on their own.

Integration Testing: Check how different layers (repositories, use cases, controllers) play together.

End-to-End (E2E) Testing: Test the whole system, from the HTTP requests all the way down to the database.

4.2 Setting Up the Testing Environment

Before we start whacking out the tests, we need to get our testing environment ready. Here's what we'll use:

Jest: Fast, easy to set up, and it works right out of the box.

Supertest: Great for testing HTTP requests, perfect for checking our Express endpoints.

Mockingoose: A library for mocking Mongoose models, so we can test without poking our real MongoDB.

Step 1: Installing Testing Dependencies

Let's install our testing tools first:

npm install --save-dev jest supertest mockingoose

Then, update the package.json to include a test script:

```
"scripts": {
  "test": "jest --coverage"
}
```

The --coverage flag is like our little secret helper, letting us know how much of the code we've covered with tests. No skimping, okay?

4.3 Unit Testing: Testing Entities and Use Cases

Unit testing is like testing your coffee order before you leave the shop, making sure it's exactly what you asked for. We're going to test small parts of our system in isolation to make sure they do their job properly.

Step 1: Unit Testing the Entity

Let's start with our UserEntity. This class holds the business logic, so we want to ensure it behaves correctly, especially when it comes to things like email validation.

Create a new folder called tests, and inside, make a file named UserEntity.test.js

```
// UserEntity.test.js

const UserEntity = require('../src/entities/UserEntity');

describe('UserEntity', () => {
  it('should create a user with valid attributes', () => {
    const user = new UserEntity({
      id: '123',
```

```
  name: 'John Doe',
  email: 'john@example.com',
  age: 30,
});

expect(user.name).toBe('John Doe');
expect(user.email).toBe('john@example.com');
});

it('should throw an error when setting an invalid email', () => {
  const user = new UserEntity({
    id: '123',
    name: 'John Doe',
    email: 'john@example.com',
    age: 30,
  });

  expect(() => user.changeEmail('invalid-email')).toThrow('Invalid email format');
});
});
```

With this, we're checking two things:

- Our entity can be set up correctly.

- The changeEmail() function properly rejects invalid emails.

To run our test, just type:

npm test

Step 2: Unit Testing the Use Case

Now, let's move on to the UserUseCases class. This time, we'll test how it talks to the user entity and the repository. But since we're focused on the use case logic here, we'll use mocks for the repository.

Create UserUseCases.test.js

```javascript
// UserUseCases.test.js

const UserUseCases = require('../src/use-cases/userUseCases');
const UserEntity = require('../src/entities/UserEntity');

describe('UserUseCases', () => {
  const mockRepository = {
    save: jest.fn(),
    findById: jest.fn(),
  };

  const useCases = new UserUseCases(mockRepository);

  it('should create a new user', async () => {
    const userData = { name: 'John Doe', email: 'john@example.com', age: 30 };
    mockRepository.save.mockResolvedValue(userData);

    const user = await useCases.createUser(userData);

    expect(mockRepository.save).toHaveBeenCalled();
    expect(user.name).toBe('John Doe');
  });

  it('should update user email', async () => {
    const user = new UserEntity({
      id: '123',
      name: 'John Doe',
      email: 'john@example.com',
      age: 30,
    });
    mockRepository.findById.mockResolvedValue(user);
    mockRepository.save.mockResolvedValue(user);
```

```
    const updatedUser = await useCases.updateUserEmail('123',
'new.email@example.com');

    expect(updatedUser.email).toBe('new.email@example.com');
  });
});
```

Here, we're making sure that:

- A new user can be created with the createUser method.

- Updating the user's email works as expected.

We're mocking the save and findById methods from the repository so we don't have to bother with real database calls. It's like testing in our own playground.

4.4 Integration Testing: Testing Repositories and Controllers

Okay, we've got the basics down, but how do we know our different parts work well together? That's where integration testing comes in. We'll test how our repositories interact with MongoDB and how our controllers handle HTTP requests.

Step 1: Testing Repositories with Mockingoose

When testing repositories, we don't want to hit the real database. That's where Mockingoose comes in handy, it helps us simulate the MongoDB interactions.

Create userRepository.test.js

```
// userRepository.test.js

const mockingoose = require('mockingoose');
const UserModel = require('../src/models/User');
const UserRepository = require('../src/repositories/userRepository');

describe('UserRepository', () => {
  const repository = new UserRepository();

  it('should find a user by ID', async () => {
```

```
  const mockUser = { _id: '123', name: 'John Doe', email: 'john@example.com',
age: 30 };
  mockingoose(UserModel).toReturn(mockUser, 'findOne');

  const user = await repository.findById('123');

  expect(user.name).toBe('John Doe');
  expect(user.email).toBe('john@example.com');
 });

 it('should save a user', async () => {
  const userEntity = { id: '123', name: 'John Doe', email: 'john@example.com', age:
30 };
  mockingoose(UserModel).toReturn(userEntity, 'save');

  const savedUser = await repository.save(userEntity);

  expect(savedUser.name).toBe('John Doe');
  expect(savedUser.email).toBe('john@example.com');
 });
});
```

With Mockingoose, we can test our repository's behavior without needing an actual MongoDB connection. Easy peasy, right?

Step 2: Testing Controllers with Supertest

Now, let's test our controllers. We want to make sure that our HTTP routes are working as expected. **Supertest** is great for simulating HTTP requests.

Create userController.test.js

```
// userController.test.js

const request = require('supertest');

const express = require('express');
const userController = require('../src/controllers/userController');
```

```javascript
const mockingoose = require('mockingoose');
const UserModel = require('../src/models/User');
const app = express();
app.use(express.json());
app.post('/users', userController.createUser);
app.put('/users/:id/email', userController.updateUserEmail);
app.get('/users', userController.getAllUsers);

describe('UserController', () => {
  it('should create a user', async () => {
    const mockUser = { _id: '123', name: 'John Doe', email: 'john@example.com',
age: 30 };
    mockingoose(UserModel).toReturn(mockUser, 'save');

    const response = await request(app)
      .post('/users')
      .send({ name: 'John Doe', email: 'john@example.com', age: 30 });

    expect(response.status).toBe(201);
    expect(response.body.name).toBe('John Doe');
  });

  it('should update user email', async () => {
    const mockUser = { _id: '123', name: 'John Doe', email: 'john@example.com',
age: 30 };
    mockingoose(UserModel).toReturn(mockUser, 'findOne');

    const response = await request(app)
      .put('/users/123/email')
      .send({ email: 'new.email@example.com' });

    expect(response.status).toBe(200);
    expect(response.body.email).toBe('new.email@example.com');
```

```
    });
});
```

With this test, we:

- Use Supertest to simulate HTTP POST and PUT requests.

- Mock Mongoose to avoid hitting a real database.

- Ensure our endpoints return the correct status codes and response bodies.

4.5 End-to-End Testing (E2E)

E2E tests are like doing a full dress rehearsal for a performance. We'll test our entire system, from the HTTP request to the database and back.

For simplicity, E2E tests are usually run with a real database (we can use Docker for that). Here's a quick example:

```
// userRoutes.test.js

const request = require('supertest');
const app = require('../src/index');  // This is our main app, with MongoDB running

describe('E2E Tests', () => {
  it('should create and retrieve a user', async () => {
    const user = { name: 'John Doe', email: 'john@example.com', age: 30 };

    // Create user
    const postResponse = await request(app)
      .post('/users')
      .send(user);

    expect(postResponse.status).toBe(201);
    expect(postResponse.body.name).toBe('John Doe');

    // Get all users
    const getResponse = await request(app).get('/users');
    expect(getResponse.status).toBe(200);
```

```
    expect(getResponse.body.length).toBe(1);
  });
});
```

Summary

We've learned how to test our Clean Architecture from different angles:

- **Unit Tests**: For testing isolated logic like entities and use cases.

- **Integration Tests**: To ensure our repositories and controllers work smoothly together.

- **End-to-End Tests**: To check that the whole system behaves as expected from request to response.

Testing helps us keep our Clean Architecture solid, reliable, and ready for anything. Next up, we'll dive into refactoring and making our architecture ready for real-world challenges like authentication, logging, and scaling up for production.

CHAPTER 5
EXTENDING CLEAN ARCHITECTURE- ADDING AUTHENTICATION AND MIDDLEWARE

Hey there, fellow devs! By now, we've built a sturdy foundation for our Node.js and MongoDB app using the principles of Clean Architecture. But like any good developer, we know there's always room for improvement. So, let's take our app up a notch by adding two essential features that every real-world app needs, **authentication** and **middleware**.

In this chapter, we're going to dig into how we can integrate **JWT-based authentication** and sprinkle in some middleware (think logging, error handling, and more), all while keeping our Clean Architecture intact.

Imagine our app as a polite and well-structured house, now we're giving it a security system to keep out unwanted guests, a logbook to keep track of every visitor, and a friendly receptionist to handle mishaps gracefully. Ready? Let's dive in and make our app a bit more "street-smart."

5.1 Why Middleware is Important in Clean Architecture

Middleware in Express is like the security guards in our app's bouncer squad, they decide whether a request gets through or gets bounced out based on certain criteria. In the context of Clean Architecture, middleware ensures that before any request makes it to our controllers (and eventually our use cases), it's already been vetted, authenticated, and logged, if needed.

Here's what we're covering when it comes to middleware:

1. **Authentication Middleware**: Verifying user identities using JWT tokens.

2. **Error Handling Middleware**: Ensuring errors are caught and handled gracefully.

3. **Logging Middleware**: Keeping a detailed record of the requests flowing through our system.

5.2 JWT-Based Authentication

Let's talk authentication. Think of it as checking IDs at a fancy club. JSON Web Tokens (JWT) are our go-to method for handling authentication in modern apps, they're like digital entry passes that users carry around once they've logged in, letting us know they're legit.

Step 1: Installing Authentication Dependencies

First things first, we'll need some packages to handle JWT authentication. Let's get these installed:

npm install jsonwebtoken bcryptjs

- jsonwebtoken: Helps us generate and verify JWTs, our digital entry passes.
- bcryptjs: Helps us securely hash and compare passwords, ensuring no one sneaks in with a weak password.

Step 2: Creating the Authentication Use Case

As with everything in Clean Architecture, we want our authentication logic to sit snugly within our use cases. This keeps our business logic separate from the delivery and data layers.

Create a new file, src/use-cases/authUseCases.js

```
// authUseCases.js

const bcrypt = require('bcryptjs');
const jwt = require('jsonwebtoken');

class AuthUseCases {
  constructor(userRepository) {
    this.userRepository = userRepository;
  }

  async registerUser(userData) {
```

```
    const hashedPassword = await bcrypt.hash(userData.password, 10);
    userData.password = hashedPassword;

    const user = await this.userRepository.save(userData);
    return user;
  }

  async loginUser(email, password) {
    const user = await this.userRepository.findByEmail(email);

    if (!user) throw new Error('User not found');

    const isPasswordValid = await bcrypt.compare(password, user.password);
    if (!isPasswordValid) throw new Error('Invalid credentials');

    const token = jwt.sign({ id: user._id, email: user.email },
process.env.JWT_SECRET, {
      expiresIn: '1h',
    });

    return { token, user };
  }

  verifyToken(token) {
    try {
      return jwt.verify(token, process.env.JWT_SECRET);
    } catch (err) {
      throw new Error('Invalid token');
    }
  }
}

module.exports = AuthUseCases;
```

Here's what's happening in our use case:

- **Registers a new user** by hashing their password for security.

- **Logs in a user** by verifying credentials and creating a JWT token for them.

- **Verifies the JWT token** to ensure that users are who they say they are.

Step 3: Creating the Authentication Middleware

Now, we'll create middleware that checks for a valid JWT token before allowing access to certain routes. Middleware like this lives in the "Framework & Drivers" layer, as it directly interacts with Express.

Create src/middleware/authMiddleware.js

```
// authMiddleware.js

const authUseCases = require('../use-cases/authUseCases');

const authMiddleware = (req, res, next) => {
  const token = req.headers['authorization'];

  if (!token) {
    return res.status(401).json({ message: 'No token provided' });
  }

  try {
    const decoded = authUseCases.verifyToken(token.split(' ')[1]);
    req.user = decoded; // Attach the decoded user info to the request object
    next();
  } catch (error) {
    res.status(401).json({ message: 'Invalid token' });
  }
};

module.exports = authMiddleware;
```

This piece of code ensures that if a request is missing a token, it's shown the door with a 401 Unauthorized status. If the token is valid, it lets the request through.

5.3 Creating the Authentication Controller

Time to build a controller that handles registration and login, our entry point for these operations.

Create src/controllers/authController.js

```
// authController.js

const authUseCases = require('../use-cases/authUseCases');
const userRepository = require('../repositories/userRepository');

const register = async (req, res) => {
  try {
    const user = await authUseCases.registerUser(req.body);
    res.status(201).json(user);
  } catch (err) {
    res.status(400).json({ message: err.message });
  }
};

const login = async (req, res) => {
  try {
    const { email, password } = req.body;
    const { token, user } = await authUseCases.loginUser(email, password);
    res.status(200).json({ token, user });
  } catch (err) {
    res.status(400).json({ message: err.message });
  }
};

module.exports = {
  register,
```

login,
};

Here's what our controller does:

- **User Registration**: Takes care of hashing passwords and storing new users.
- **User Login**: Checks credentials and hands back a shiny new JWT token if they check out.

Step 4: Updating Routes

We'll add routes for registration and login, and secure some routes with our authentication middleware.

Update src/index.js

```
// index.js

const express = require('express');
const mongoose = require('mongoose');
const authController = require('./controllers/authController');
const userController = require('./controllers/userController');
const authMiddleware = require('./middleware/authMiddleware');

const app = express();
app.use(express.json());

mongoose.connect(process.env.MONGO_URI, { useNewUrlParser: true,
useUnifiedTopology: true })
  .then(() => console.log('MongoDB connected'))
  .catch((err) => console.error('MongoDB connection error:', err));

// Authentication routes
app.post('/auth/register', authController.register);
app.post('/auth/login', authController.login);

// Secure routes with authentication middleware
app.get('/users', authMiddleware, userController.getAllUsers);
```

```
app.put('/users/:id/email', authMiddleware, userController.updateUserEmail);
```

```
const port = process.env.PORT || 3000;
app.listen(port, () => console.log(`Server running on port ${port}`));
```

Now we've got registration and login routes, and our /users routes are protected with authMiddleware. Only users with a valid JWT token can access those.

5.4 Logging Middleware

Logging is like our app's diary, it keeps track of everything happening, from user actions to system events. Let's create a simple logging middleware to keep tabs on every request.

Create src/middleware/loggerMiddleware.js

```
// loggerMiddleware.js
const loggerMiddleware = (req, res, next) => {
  console.log(`${new Date().toISOString()} - ${req.method} ${req.originalUrl}`);
  next(); // Pass control to the next middleware or controller
};
```

```
module.exports = loggerMiddleware;
```
And add it to index.js:
```
const loggerMiddleware = require('./middleware/loggerMiddleware');
```

```
app.use(loggerMiddleware);  // Apply logging middleware globally
```

With this, our app now logs every request method and URL. A simple but effective way to keep an eye on things!

5.5 Error Handling Middleware

Nobody likes surprises, especially when it comes to errors. With error-handling middleware, we can catch those surprises and respond gracefully.

Create src/middleware/errorMiddleware.js

```
// errorMiddleware.js
```

```js
const errorMiddleware = (err, req, res, next) => {

  console.error(err.stack);  // Log the error stack for debugging

  res.status(500).json({ message: 'Something went wrong!' });

};
```

```js
module.exports = errorMiddleware;
```

And hook it up in index.js:

```js
// index.js

const errorMiddleware = require('./middleware/errorMiddleware');

app.use(errorMiddleware);  // Error handling should be the last middleware
```

This middleware catches any unhandled errors, logs them, and sends back a generic error message.

5.6 Testing Authentication

Let's make sure our authentication works as expected with **Supertest**.

Create tests/authController.test.js

```js
// authController.test.js

const request = require('supertest');
const mongoose = require('mongoose');
const app = require('../index'); // Assuming your Express app is exported in index.js
const User = require('../models/User'); // Adjust the path based on your project
structure

describe('Auth Controller', () => {
  beforeAll(async () => {
    // Connect to a test database
    await mongoose.connect(process.env.TEST_MONGO_URI, { useNewUrlParser:
true, useUnifiedTopology: true });
  });

  afterAll(async () => {
    // Clean up and disconnect from the database
```

```
  await User.deleteMany({});
  await mongoose.disconnect();
});

describe('POST /auth/register', () => {
  it('should register a new user and return 201 status', async () => {
    const newUser = {
      email: 'test@example.com',
      password: 'password123',
    };

    const res = await request(app).post('/auth/register').send(newUser);

    expect(res.status).toBe(201);
    expect(res.body).toHaveProperty('_id');
    expect(res.body.email).toBe(newUser.email);
  });

  it('should return 400 if the email already exists', async () => {
    const duplicateUser = {
      email: 'test@example.com',
      password: 'password123',
    };

    const res = await request(app).post('/auth/register').send(duplicateUser);

    expect(res.status).toBe(400);
        expect(res.body.message).toBe('User already exists'); // Customize message
based on your implementation
  });
});

describe('POST /auth/login', () => {
  it('should login a user and return a token', async () => {
    const user = {
```

```
    email: 'test@example.com',
    password: 'password123',
  };

  const res = await request(app).post('/auth/login').send(user);

  expect(res.status).toBe(200);
  expect(res.body).toHaveProperty('token');
  expect(res.body.user.email).toBe(user.email);
});

it('should return 400 if credentials are invalid', async () => {
  const invalidUser = {
    email: 'test@example.com',
    password: 'wrongpassword',
  };

  const res = await request(app).post('/auth/login').send(invalidUser);

  expect(res.status).toBe(400);
      expect(res.body.message).toBe('Invalid credentials'); // Customize message
based on your implementation
  });

it('should return 400 if the user does not exist', async () => {
  const nonExistentUser = {
    email: 'nonexistent@example.com',
    password: 'password123',
  };

  const res = await request(app).post('/auth/login').send(nonExistentUser);

  expect(res.status).toBe(400);
    expect(res.body.message).toBe('User not found'); // Customize message based
on your implementation
```

```
    });
  });
});
```

This test suite ensures our registration and login processes are airtight and error-proof.

Summary

We've just extended our Clean Architecture app with powerful authentication and middleware capabilities. In this chapter, we covered:

- **JWT Authentication**: How to securely register and log in users.

- **Middleware**: Managing authentication, logging, and error handling like a pro.

- **Testing Authentication**: Making sure our authentication logic is robust.

CHAPTER 6
IMPLEMENTING REPOSITORIES WITH MONGODB

In this chapter we're kicking things up a notch! Imagine if Clean Architecture was a movie, then the **Repository** would be the smooth, undercover agent working behind the scenes, fetching data without getting entangled in the drama. It's like our trusty sidekick, keeping our domain logic blissfully unaware of where the data comes from, be it MongoDB, PostgreSQL, or maybe even an Excel sheet (ok, maybe not Excel, but you catch my drift).

In this chapter, we're going to:

Get cozy with the **Repository pattern** and its role in Clean Architecture. Implement it in **Node.js**, with **MongoDB** as our database of choice. Tackle advanced query magic like pagination, filtering, and aggregation. Make sure our repositories are designed with best practices in mind. Learn how to mock repositories in tests, keeping our unit tests fast and fuss-free.

6.1 Introduction to Repositories in Clean Architecture

The **Repository pattern** is all about keeping things nice and abstract. Imagine you've got some data that needs to be accessed, but you don't want your core logic poking around in the database itself. Instead, you create a **repository interface**, a clean little interface that provides methods to fetch, save, update, or delete data.

This approach keeps our domain logic blissfully unaware of how or where the data is actually stored. In Clean Architecture, repositories live in the **interface adapter layer**, acting as intermediaries between use cases and databases.

A simple analogy: imagine a repository as a waiter in your favorite hawker centre. You (the use case) give your order, and the waiter (the repository) heads to the kitchen (the database) to get your food. You don't care if the chef is using a wok or a grill, you just want your delicious plate of char kway teow.

6.2 Implementing Repository Pattern in Node.js

Alright, let's set up a solid foundation for our repositories.

Creating Interfaces for Data Access Layer

First, we need to define the interface (or "contract") that our repository must follow. Now, JavaScript doesn't come with native interfaces like some other languages (think Java or C#), but we can still create an abstract class or document the methods we expect.

Here's what a **UserRepository interface** might look like in JavaScript:

```
// src/repositories/UserRepository.js

class UserRepository {
  async findById(id) {
    throw new Error('Method not implemented.');
  }

  async save(user) {
    throw new Error('Method not implemented.');
  }

  async update(user) {
    throw new Error('Method not implemented.');
  }

  async deleteById(id) {
    throw new Error('Method not implemented.');
  }

  async findAll() {
    throw new Error('Method not implemented.');
  }
}
module.exports = UserRepository;
```

This defines the "contract" for our repository. Any concrete implementation, like one for MongoDB, needs to fulfill this contract.

Concrete Implementations for MongoDB Using Mongoose

Now, let's bring in **Mongoose** and create a MongoDB implementation of our UserRepository.

Start by installing **Mongoose**:

npm install mongoose

Next, we'll create the actual MongoDB implementation of our UserRepository

```
// src/repositories/mongoose/MongoUserRepository.js

const UserRepository = require('./UserRepository');
const UserModel = require('../models/User'); // Mongoose model

class MongoUserRepository extends UserRepository {
  async findById(id) {
    return UserModel.findById(id);
  }

  async save(userData) {
    const user = new UserModel(userData);
    return user.save();
  }

  async update(user) {
    return UserModel.findByIdAndUpdate(user._id, user, { new: true });
  }

  async deleteById(id) {
    return UserModel.findByIdAndDelete(id);
  }

  async findAll() {
```

```
    return UserModel.find();
  }
}
module.exports = MongoUserRepository;
```

What's going on here?

- We're using **Mongoose** to connect with MongoDB. Each method in our repository maps to a corresponding Mongoose operation.

- We've abstracted away the database access behind the repository, so our core logic doesn't have to worry about MongoDB's quirks.

Here's the Mongoose **User model** for context:

```
// src/models/User.js

const mongoose = require('mongoose');

const userSchema = new mongoose.Schema({
  name: { type: String, required: true },
  email: { type: String, required: true, unique: true },
  password: { type: String, required: true },
  age: { type: Number },
});

const UserModel = mongoose.model('User', userSchema);
module.exports = UserModel;
```

And that's it! We've got ourselves a **MongoDB repository** using Mongoose. Shiok, right?

6.3 Handling Query Logic

Repositories aren't just for CRUD (Create, Read, Update, Delete), sometimes we need them to perform more complex queries. Let's explore how to do this with MongoDB:

Complex Queries and Aggregation in MongoDB

MongoDB is super flexible for handling complex queries. Let's say we want to find users above 18 with a certain email domain:

```
async findAdultsWithEmailDomain(domain) {
  return UserModel.find({
    age: { $gt: 18 },
    email: { $regex: new RegExp(`${domain}$`, 'i') }
  });
}
```

In this query:

- We're finding users older than 18 (age: { $gt: 18 }).

- We use a regular expression to match emails ending with a specific domain.

Aggregation is another powerful feature. For example, if we want to calculate the **average age of users** grouped by their email domains:

```
async getAverageAgeByEmailDomain() {
  return UserModel.aggregate([
    { $group: { _id: { $substr: ['$email', { $indexOfBytes: ["$email", "@"] }, -1] },
avgAge: { $avg: '$age' } } }
  ]);
}
```

This query groups users by their email domains and calculates the average age for each group. Like magic, but with code!

Pagination, Filtering, and Sorting

When our user database starts growing, pagination helps manage large datasets. MongoDB makes this easy with .limit() and .skip():

```
async findUsersWithPagination(page, limit, minAge) {
  const skip = (page - 1) * limit;
  return UserModel.find({ age: { $gte: minAge } })
    .sort({ name: 1 }) // Sort by name in ascending order
```

```
    .skip(skip)
    .limit(limit);
}
```

This snippet helps us paginate through users:

- skip tells MongoDB how many records to skip.

- limit restricts the number of users returned per page. sort sorts users by name alphabetically.

6.4 Best Practices for Repository Design

Building repositories well is like cooking laksa, get the right balance, and everything flows smoothly. Here are some best practices:

1. Keep Repositories Dumb

Repositories should stick to their job: **data access**. Business logic? That's for the **use cases**.

2. Don't Make a Swiss Army Knife

Each repository should focus on one entity (e.g., UserRepository for user data). If your repository starts looking like a rojak, it's time to break it up into smaller, focused repositories.

3. Use Dependency Injection

By injecting repository interfaces, our use cases don't have to care whether it's MongoDB or another database behind the scenes. This keeps our architecture flexible.

4. Optimize Queries

Index your collections and write efficient queries to avoid slow database operations. No one likes a laggy app, right?

5. Handle Errors Gracefully

Always catch errors from database operations. If MongoDB's having a bad day, make sure our app returns friendly error messages.

6.5 Mocking Repositories for Unit Testing

When writing unit tests, we want to avoid hitting the database directly, that's what **integration tests** are for. For unit tests, we'll **mock** the repository to return controlled test data.

Here's how we can mock our UserRepository in a test for a use case

```
// UserRepository.test.js

const { findUserUseCase } = require('../src/use-cases/findUserUseCase');
const UserRepository = require('../src/repositories/UserRepository');

describe('FindUserUseCase', () => {
  it('should return a user by ID', async () => {
    const mockUser = { id: '123', name: 'John Doe', email: 'john@example.com' };

    // Mock the repository method
    const mockRepository = new UserRepository();
    mockRepository.findById = jest.fn().mockResolvedValue(mockUser);

    // Call the use case
    const user = await findUserUseCase(mockRepository, '123');

    // Assertions
    expect(mockRepository.findById).toHaveBeenCalledWith('123');
    expect(user).toEqual(mockUser);
  });
});
```

By mocking UserRepository, our tests remain fast and focused on the business logic, not the database.

Summary

We covered the **Repository pattern** and its role in Clean Architecture. Building repositories with **MongoDB** and **Mongoose**. Complex queries, pagination, filtering, and sorting. Best practices to keep our repositories clean and efficient. How to mock repositories for smooth unit testing.

CHAPTER 7
BUILDING INTERFACE ADAPTERS (FOR DEVS, BY DEVS)

In this chapter, we're diving into the world of **Interface Adapters**. These are like those super-talented interpreters who make sure everyone's on the same page, whether it's handling HTTP requests, talking to a database, or getting your app's core logic ready for the outside world. Think of them as the "middlemen", but way cooler and more essential to our app's success.

By the time we wrap this chapter, we'll have our hands dirty with controllers, data validation, and integrating MongoDB in a way that's both clean and fun to work with. And yes, we'll also throw in some **presenters** to make sure our data is nicely packaged before it heads out to the client.

Ready? Let's go!

7.1 Role of Interface Adapters in Clean Architecture

In Clean Architecture, the **Interface Adapters** layer is our trusty translator, taking data from the outside (like HTTP requests or database queries) and converting it into something our core app logic (the use cases and entities) can work with. And of course, it works the other way around too, sending clean, structured data back out to the external world.

Converting Between Internal and External Models

Our internal logic doesn't care if the data comes from an HTTP request, a database, or a magical data source, it just wants its data in a specific format. That's where Interface Adapters come in. They convert incoming data into a shape our use cases can understand, and then convert results back into a format ready for the client.

Here's the lowdown:

- **External input (e.g., HTTP request)** ➔ Adapted into a model for our use cases.

- **Internal output (e.g., use case result)** ➔ Adapted into a client-friendly format (e.g., a JSON response).

Picture this: Our app is a fancy Singaporean restaurant. The **Interface Adapters** are like the service staff. They take customer orders (incoming HTTP requests), deliver them to the chefs (use cases), and bring out the delicious meals (responses) without the kitchen ever having to deal directly with the diners. Efficient, right?

Data Transfer Objects (DTOs) and Mapping Strategies

Let's talk about **Data Transfer Objects (DTOs)**, the workhorses that carry data back and forth between our app layers. In the Interface Adapter layer, DTOs define what data is coming into and out of our system.

Why use DTOs?

- **Decoupling**: DTOs keep our internal domain model isolated from external data structures like API requests.

- **Validation**: DTOs make it easy to validate the data coming in and going out.

- **Clarity**: They make it crystal clear what data is expected and what's being returned.

Here's a simple **UserDTO** for creating a user:

```
// src/dto/UserDTO.js

class UserDTO {
  constructor({ name, email, password, age }) {
    this.name = name;
    this.email = email;
    this.password = password;
    this.age = age;
  }
}

module.exports = UserDTO;
```

Mapping Strategy:

- **Incoming Data**: Map HTTP request data into a DTO.

- **Outgoing Data**: Map internal results into an external format (like JSON).

7.2 Implementing Controllers in Node.js

RESTful API Design Principles

Before we jump into building controllers, let's quickly refresh the core principles of **RESTful API design**:

1. **Stateless**: Every request from the client needs to carry all the info the server needs to handle it.

2. **Resources**: Everything in REST is a resource, accessed via URIs (e.g., / users).

3. **HTTP Methods**:

   1.1.**GET**: Grab data.

   1.2.**POST**: Create something new.

   1.3.**PUT/PATCH**: Update existing data.

   1.4.**DELETE**: Remove stuff.

4. **Status Codes**: Always return the right status codes (e.g., 200 OK, 201 Created, 400 Bad Request, 404 Not Found).

Creating Routes and Controllers Using Express.js

In Node.js, our **controllers** handle HTTP requests, call the right use cases, and return the right responses. Let's whip up a controller for managing users using **Express.js**.

Step 1: Setting Up Routes

First, create a router for user-related endpoints in src/routes/userRoutes.js

```
// src/routes/userRoutes.js

const express = require('express');
```

```
const router = express.Router();
const userController = require('../controllers/userController');
```

```
// Define routes
router.get('/', userController.getAllUsers);
router.post('/', userController.createUser);
router.put('/:id', userController.updateUser);
router.delete('/:id', userController.deleteUser);
```

```
module.exports = router;
```

Step 2: Implementing the User Controller

Now let's build the actual controller to handle our routes. This is where we map HTTP requests to DTOs and pass them to our use cases.

Create src/controllers/userController.js

```
// src/controllers/userController.js
```

```
const userUseCases = require('../use-cases/userUseCases');
const UserDTO = require('../dto/UserDTO');
```

```
const getAllUsers = async (req, res) => {
  try {
    const users = await userUseCases.getAllUsers();
    res.status(200).json({ data: users });
  } catch (err) {
    res.status(500).json({ error: err.message });
  }
};
```

```
const createUser = async (req, res) => {
  try {
    const userDTO = new UserDTO(req.body);
    const newUser = await userUseCases.createUser(userDTO);
    res.status(201).json({ data: newUser });
```

```javascript
} catch (err) {
  res.status(400).json({ error: err.message });
  }
};

const updateUser = async (req, res) => {
  try {
    const userDTO = new UserDTO({ ...req.body, id: req.params.id });
    const updatedUser = await userUseCases.updateUser(userDTO);
    res.status(200).json({ data: updatedUser });
  } catch (err) {
    res.status(400).json({ error: err.message });
  }
};

const deleteUser = async (req, res) => {
  try {
    await userUseCases.deleteUser(req.params.id);
    res.status(204).send(); // 204 means "No Content"
  } catch (err) {
    res.status(404).json({ error: err.message });
  }
};

module.exports = {
  getAllUsers,
  createUser,
  updateUser,
  deleteUser,
};
```

In this controller, we're:

- Accepting HTTP requests, mapping them to **DTOs**, and passing them to the right use cases.

- Returning responses with proper HTTP status codes.

- Handling errors so our users get clear messages when something goes wrong.

7.3 Handling HTTP Requests and Responses

Request Validation with Middleware (e.g., Joi, Express-validator)

To make sure incoming requests are legit, we'll add validation using **Joi**.

First, install **Joi**:

npm install joi

Create a validation middleware for user creation in src/middleware/validateUser.js:

```
// src/middleware/validateUser.js:

const Joi = require('joi');

const validateUser = (req, res, next) => {
  const schema = Joi.object({
    name: Joi.string().min(3).required(),
    email: Joi.string().email().required(),
    password: Joi.string().min(6).required(),
    age: Joi.number().min(18).optional(),
  });

  const { error } = schema.validate(req.body);

  if (error) {
    return res.status(400).json({ error: error.details[0].message });
  }

  next(); // Move on if validation is all good
};


module.exports = validateUser;
```

Use this middleware in your routes:

```
const validateUser = require('../middleware/validateUser');

router.post('/', validateUser, userController.createUser);
```

With this, if a user sends a bad request to the /users endpoint, our middleware will catch it and return a 400 Bad Request error.

Response Formats and Error Handling

Consistency is key. So let's ensure that our API responses always follow the same format:

- **Success**: { "data": ... }
- **Error**: { "error": "message" }

For example, tweak your controller to return responses like this:

```
// src/controllers/userController.js
const createUser = async (req, res) => {
  try {
    const userDTO = new UserDTO(req.body);
    const newUser = await userUseCases.createUser(userDTO);
    res.status(201).json({ data: newUser });
  } catch (err) {
    res.status(400).json({ error: err.message });
  }
};
```

7.4 Adapter Layer for MongoDB Interaction

In Clean Architecture, the **repository layer** connects our core business logic with our data source (like MongoDB). Our use cases don't care whether the data's from MongoDB, SQL, or a JSON file, they just want the data.

We've already built a MongoUserRepository in Chapter 6. Here's a quick look at how it fits into the Interface Adapter layer

```
// src/use-cases/userUseCases.js
const createUser = async (userDTO) => {
  return

  userRepository.save(userDTO); // Our use case doesn't care that MongoDB is
behind this!
};

module.exports = {
  createUser,
  getAllUsers,
  updateUser,
  deleteUser,
};
```

This separation means that if we switch databases later, our core logic stays the same. Neat, right?

7.5 Implementing Presenters

Presenters are like translators, converting internal models into data formats the outside world understands. For REST APIs, that means taking our models and turning them into clean, well-formatted JSON.

Create a src/presenters/UserPresenter.js

```
// src/presenters/UserPresenter.js
class UserPresenter {
  static toJson(user) {
    return {
      id: user._id,
      name: user.name,
      email: user.email,
      age: user.age,
    };
  }
}
```

```
static toJsonMany(users) {
  return users.map(UserPresenter.toJson);
  }
}
module.exports = UserPresenter;
```

Use the presenter in your controller to format responses

```
// src/controllers/userController.js
const UserPresenter = require('../presenters/UserPresenter');
const getAllUsers = async (req, res) => {
  try {
    const users = await userUseCases.getAllUsers();
    res.status(200).json({ data: UserPresenter.toJsonMany(users) });
  } catch (err) {
    res.status(500).json({ error: err.message });
  }
};
```

Now, no matter what changes behind the scenes, our clients get consistent, clean JSON responses.

Summary

We've just explored the **Interface Adapters** layer, and it's been a wild ride through handling data like a pro. Here we have covered how **Interface Adapters** convert data between our app's core logic and the outside world using **DTOs**. Implementing **controllers** and **RESTful routes** with Express. Using middleware like Joi for **request validation** and **error handling**. Using repositories to keep our MongoDB logic separate from the use cases. Finally, building **presenters** to make sure responses are always nicely formatted.

CHAPTER 8
DEPENDENCY INJECTION AND INVERSION OF CONTROL

In this Chapter, we dive into two heavy-hitters of software architecture, **Dependency Injection (DI)** and **Inversion of Control (IoC)**. These are like the directors behind the scenes of a blockbuster movie, making sure the actors (yup, that's our app components) interact smoothly without getting tangled up in each other's business.

Think of DI and IoC as your ticket to building apps that are as flexible as a Singaporean food court menu, decoupled like a well-oiled Lego set, and ready for the limelight when it comes to testing.

By the end of this chapter, we'll cover:

1. What **Dependency Injection** is and how to use it effectively.
2. How **Inversion of Control** flips the script, giving control over to the infrastructure.
3. Implementing DI in a **Node.js** app using **Awilix**.
4. How DI keeps our Clean Architecture, well, clean, testable, and maintainable.

Grab a coffee, sit back, and let's go deep into the world of DI and IoC!

8.1 What's Dependency Injection (DI)?

So, what exactly is this DI thing? It sounds fancy, but at its core, DI is just a way to give a class or function the things (dependencies) it needs, without it having to go out and create them itself.

Think of it this way: imagine you're at our favourite kopitiam (coffee shop), and instead of you brewing your own coffee, the friendly barista hands you a freshly made cup. In this analogy, **you** (the class) don't need to know how to brew the coffee (create the dependency). The barista (our DI container) takes care of the brewing, handing you the finished product when you need it.

This pattern has a few key benefits.

Key Benefits of Dependency Injection

1. **Decoupling**: Classes don't have to know the details of how dependencies are made; they just use them.
2. **Testability**: It's easy to swap out dependencies during testing, perfect for mocking or stubbing.
3. **Flexibility**: Need to swap out MongoDB for PostgreSQL? Just update it in one spot instead of hunting down all the places it's used.

8.2 Understanding Inversion of Control (IoC)

Now, let's chat about Inversion of Control (IoC). If DI is the act of passing dependencies, IoC is the philosophy that makes it all possible. Normally, our code is the boss, it creates objects, decides how to use them, and handles everything. But IoC says, "Hey, let the framework or infrastructure handle that stuff." It flips the control, so your code just asks for what it needs.

Picture yourself as a busy executive, you could book your own Grab rides, but why not have a personal assistant do it for you? IoC is like that assistant, arranging everything so you can focus on more important stuff.

Here's a quick visual to show how it changes the flow:

Traditional Approach: IoC Approach:

```
+-----------------------------+        +-----------------------------+
|        Service Class        |        |        Service Class        |
|-----------------------------|        |-----------------------------|
|   - Creates dependencies    |        |   - Requests dependencies|
|   - Calls methods itself    |        |   - DI Container provides|
+-----------------------------+        +-----------------------------+
            ^                                        v
+-----------------------------+        +-----------------------------+
|    Dependency Container      |        |    Dependency Container      |
|-----------------------------|        |-----------------------------|
|   - Provides dependencies|           |   - Injects dependencies |
+-----------------------------+        +-----------------------------+
```

8.3 Hands-On with Dependency Injection in Node.js

Now it's time to roll up our sleeves and implement DI in a Node.js app using **Awilix**, a neat DI container that plays well with Express.

Step 1: Install Awilix

First, let's get Awilix up and running:

npm install awilix awilix-express

- **awilix**: The core DI container.

- **awilix-express**: Integrates smoothly with Express, making dependency injection into controllers a breeze.

Step 2: Setting Up the DI Container

Now, let's create a file called container.js where we'll set up our DI container and register all the dependencies.

```
// src/container.js

const { createContainer, asClass, asFunction } = require('awilix');
const UserRepository = require('./repositories/MongoUserRepository');
const UserUseCases = require('./use-cases/userUseCases');
const userController = require('./controllers/userController');

// Create a DI container
const container = createContainer();

// Register dependencies
container.register({
  userRepository: asClass(UserRepository).scoped(),
  userUseCases: asClass(UserUseCases).scoped(),
  userController: asFunction(userController).scoped(),
});

module.exports = container;
```

In this setup:

- **createContainer()**: Builds the DI container.

- **register()**: Registers dependencies, like giving the barista instructions on how to brew different types of coffee.

- **asClass** and **asFunction**: Let Awilix know whether to create class instances or function-based components.

Step 3: Refactoring Controllers with DI

Next, let's refactor our userController to receive dependencies via DI.

```
// src/controllers/userController.js
module.exports = ({ userUseCases }) => ({
 getAllUsers: async (req, res) => {
  try {
   const users = await userUseCases.getAllUsers();
   res.status(200).json({ data: users });
  } catch (err) {
   res.status(500).json({ error: err.message });
  }
 },

 createUser: async (req, res) => {
  try {
   const newUser = await userUseCases.createUser(req.body);
   res.status(201).json({ data: newUser });
  } catch (err) {
   res.status(400).json({ error: err.message });
  }
 },
});
```

Now, userController is a **function** that receives userUseCases as a dependency, and Awilix takes care of passing it in.

Step 4: Hooking Up Awilix with Express

To wire it all up, let's modify index.js to integrate Awilix with Express.

```js
// src/index.js

const express = require('express');
const { scopePerRequest } = require('awilix-express');
const userRoutes = require('./routes/userRoutes');
const container = require('./container');

const app = express();
app.use(express.json());
app.use(scopePerRequest(container));

// Define routes
app.use('/users', userRoutes);

const port = process.env.PORT || 3000;
app.listen(port, () => {
  console.log(`Server running on port ${port}`);
});
```

Step 5: Using DI in Routes

Now, we define our routes and let Awilix inject dependencies into our controllers.

```js
// src/routes/userRoutes.js

const express = require('express');
const { makeInvoker } = require('awilix-express');
const router = express.Router();
const userController = makeInvoker(require('../controllers/userController'));

router.get('/', userController('getAllUsers'));
router.post('/', userController('createUser'));

module.exports = router;
```

With **makeInvoker**, the right dependencies get injected into our controller, like a barista knowing whether to brew a latte or an espresso.

8.4 Keeping Dependencies Tidy Across Layers

The beauty of DI is how it keeps each layer of our app independent. Our UserController doesn't have to worry about how UserUseCases are created, it just asks the DI container for them. Same goes for UserUseCases when it needs the UserRepository.

This means we can tweak or swap out implementations without breaking the rest of the app, like switching out the coffee beans without needing a new coffee machine. It's all about making things modular, easier to change, and cleaner.

8.5 Testing Made Easier with DI

Testing with DI is a breeze because we can easily inject **mock** or **stub** dependencies. Let's mock out the UserUseCases in a simple test for our UserController.

```
// tests/userController.test.js

const { createUser } = require('../src/controllers/userController')({
  userUseCases: {
    createUser: jest.fn().mockResolvedValue({ id: '123', name: 'John Doe' }),
  },
});

describe('UserController', () => {
  it('should create a new user', async () => {
    const req = { body: { name: 'John Doe', email: 'john@example.com' } };
    const res = {
      status: jest.fn().mockReturnThis(),
      json: jest.fn(),
    };

    await createUser(req, res);
```

```
  expect(res.status).toHaveBeenCalledWith(201);
  expect(res.json).toHaveBeenCalledWith({ data: { id: '123', name: 'John Doe' } });
  });
});
```

In this test:

- We use jest.fn() to create a mock userUseCases.createUser.

- We simulate an HTTP request with fake req and res objects.

- Then, we verify the results using assertions.

This setup lets us focus on the controller logic without worrying about the underlying use cases, perfect for keeping our tests quick and reliable.

Summary

We've unwrapped the mysteries of **Dependency Injection (DI)** and **Inversion of Control (IoC)**, learning how they help make our apps more modular, testable, and easy to change.

Key takeaways:

1. **Dependency Injection** helps us keep classes light and easy to change.

2. **Inversion of Control** lets the infrastructure handle the heavy lifting of managing dependencies.

We implemented DI in **Node.js** using **Awilix**, learning to keep things neat from setup to integration. DI makes testing smoother by allowing us to easily mock out dependencies. With DI and IoC in place, our Clean Architecture is not just clean, it's flexible and test-friendly.

CHAPTER 9
IMPLEMENTING CROSS-CUTTING CONCERNS

Eh, welcome to **Chapter 9**, ah! Here, we're diving into a topic that's sure to spice up your software development skills, **Cross-Cutting Concerns**. Now, you might be wondering, what's that? Well, think of them as the unsung heroes of your app, features like logging, monitoring, authentication, and error handling that work across different parts of your application. They're like those silent security guards and cleaners at Changi Airport, keeping things smooth, safe, and clean behind the scenes, ah.

In this chapter, we'll show how to integrate these concerns into a **Node.js** app while staying true to **Clean Architecture** principles. Along the way, we'll be exploring how to handle logging, manage authentication, gracefully tackle errors, and more, all while keeping our code clean, modular, and manageable.

By the end of this chapter, we'll have a solid understanding of:

1. **Logging and Monitoring**: How to keep an eye on what's happening inside our app.

2. **Authentication and Authorization**: Ensuring only the right people can access certain parts.

3. **Error Handling and Validation**: Handling errors with style and validating our inputs properly.

So, let's roll up our sleeves and bring some order to the chaos, lah!

9.1 Handling Logging and Monitoring

Logging is like having a diary for our app. It records all the details, who did what, when things went wrong, and when they went right. And when something goes "lah ti lah" (messes up), those logs will save our skin, helping us trace back what went down. **Monitoring**, on the other hand, is like our coffee break supervisor, keeping an eye on the app's health and performance, so we catch issues early before they snowball.

Why Logging Matters in Clean Architecture

In **Clean Architecture**, logging is like those quiet neighbours, we don't want them making too much noise and disturbing our core business logic. That means logging needs to be handled **transparently**, without being a busybody in other parts of the app. Using middleware for logging helps us keep our code nice and tidy, not all mixed up with log statements.

Step 1: Setting Up Winston for Logging

We're going to use **Winston**, one of the go-to logging libraries for Node.js. Trust me, it's solid like MRT tracks.

First, we install Winston:

npm install winston

Then, we'll create a logger module to centralize all our logging needs

```
// src/logger.js

const { createLogger, format, transports } = require('winston');

const logger = createLogger({
  level: 'info',
  format: format.combine(
    format.timestamp(),
    format.printf(({ timestamp, level, message }) => {
      return `${timestamp} [${level.toUpperCase()}]: ${message}`;
    })
  ),
  transports: [
    new transports.Console(),
    new transports.File({ filename: 'logs/app.log' })
  ]
});
```

```
module.exports = logger;
```

In this setup:

- **Console Transport**: Logs will show up in our terminal.

- **File Transport**: Logs get saved in logs/app.log, like keeping receipts for later. The log format includes a timestamp and log level, so we always know what happened and when, ah.

Step 2: Logging Middleware

Now, we create middleware to log every incoming request, like a vigilant coffee aunty taking note of every customer

```
// src/middleware/loggerMiddleware.js

const logger = require('../logger');

const loggerMiddleware = (req, res, next) => {
  logger.info(`${req.method} ${req.originalUrl}`);
  next(); // Continue to the next middleware or route handler
};

module.exports = loggerMiddleware;
```

Step 3: Applying the Logging Middleware

To make sure every request is logged, we add this middleware in our index.js

```
// src/index.js

const express = require('express');
const loggerMiddleware = require('./middleware/loggerMiddleware');
const userRoutes = require('./routes/userRoutes');

const app = express();
app.use(express.json());

// Apply logging middleware
```

```
app.use(loggerMiddleware);

// User routes
app.use('/users', userRoutes);

const port = process.env.PORT || 3000;
app.listen(port, () => {
  console.log(`Server running on port ${port}`);
});
```

With this, every request to our app will be logged, both in our terminal and in app.log. It's like having CCTV cameras for our server, so when something fishy happens, we can easily playback and see.

Monitoring with Prometheus

Logging's great, but we need monitoring too, like our own mini HDB flat surveillance. For this, we'll use **Prometheus**, a popular open-source tool for monitoring apps.

First, let's install the **prom-client** library:

npm install prom-client

Now, we'll set up a basic monitoring endpoint

```
// src/metrics.js

const client = require('prom-client');

// Create a registry for metrics
const register = new client.Registry();

// Add default metrics like HTTP requests and memory usage
client.collectDefaultMetrics({ register });

// Custom counter for HTTP requests
const httpRequestCounter = new client.Counter({
```

```
  name: 'http_requests_total',
  help: 'Total number of HTTP requests',
  labelNames: ['method', 'route', 'status']
});

register.registerMetric(httpRequestCounter);

module.exports = { register, httpRequestCounter };
```

Then, create middleware to count HTTP requests

```
// src/middleware/metricsMiddleware.js

const { httpRequestCounter } = require('../metrics');

const metricsMiddleware = (req, res, next) => {
  res.on('finish', () => {
    httpRequestCounter.inc({
      method: req.method,
      route: req.originalUrl,
      status: res.statusCode
    });
  });
  next();
};

module.exports = metricsMiddleware;
```

Finally, we expose a /metrics endpoint for Prometheus to collect data

```
// src/index.js

const express = require('express');
const loggerMiddleware = require('./middleware/loggerMiddleware');
const metricsMiddleware = require('./middleware/metricsMiddleware');
const { register } = require('./metrics');
const userRoutes = require('./routes/userRoutes');
```

```
const app = express();
app.use(express.json());

app.use(loggerMiddleware);
app.use(metricsMiddleware);

// User routes
app.use('/users', userRoutes);

// Metrics endpoint for Prometheus
app.get('/metrics', async (req, res) => {
  res.set('Content-Type', register.contentType);
  res.end(await register.metrics());
});

const port = process.env.PORT || 3000;
app.listen(port, () => {
  console.log(`Server running on port ${port}`);
});
```

Now Prometheus can scrape the /metrics endpoint and give us insights into our app's performance, like having a fitness tracker for our server, telling us when it's working too hard.

9.2 Implementing Authentication and Authorization

Okay lah, time to secure our app with **Authentication** and **Authorization**. These two are like our NRIC and entry passes, they check who can enter and who can't. We'll set up **JWT-based authentication**, ensuring only people with the right "chops" get access to certain resources.

Step 1: Setting Up JWT Authentication

Let's create middleware that checks for a valid JWT (our digital entry pass)

// src/middleware/authMiddleware.js

```javascript
const jwt = require('jsonwebtoken');
const logger = require('../logger');

const authMiddleware = (req, res, next) => {
  const token = req.headers['authorization'];

  if (!token) {
    logger.warn('No token provided');
    return res.status(401).json({ error: 'No token provided' });
  }

  try {
    const decoded = jwt.verify(token.split(' ')[1], process.env.JWT_SECRET);
    req.user = decoded;
    next();
  } catch (error) {
    logger.warn('Invalid token');
    res.status(401).json({ error: 'Invalid token' });
  }
};

module.exports = authMiddleware;
```

This middleware checks if a token is present and valid. If everything checks out, it proceeds; if not, it blocks entry with a 401 Unauthorized.

Step 2: Applying Authentication Middleware

We use this middleware to protect our routes like a bouncer at Zouk

```javascript
// src/routes/userRoutes.js

const express = require('express');
const { makeInvoker } = require('awilix-express');
const authMiddleware = require('../middleware/authMiddleware');
const router = express.Router();
```

```
const userController = makeInvoker(require('../controllers/userController'));

router.get('/', authMiddleware, userController('getAllUsers'));
router.post('/', authMiddleware, userController('createUser'));

module.exports = router;
```

Now, anyone who wants to access the /users route needs a valid token, or they'll be denied entry.

Role-Based Authorization

Now, let's get fancy with **Role-Based Authorization**. This is like having a VIP area, only certain roles can access certain routes.

```
// src/middleware/roleMiddleware.js

const roleMiddleware = (requiredRole) => {
  return (req, res, next) => {
    if (req.user && req.user.role === requiredRole) {
      next();
    } else {
      res.status(403).json({ error: 'Forbidden: Insufficient permissions' });
    }
  };
};

module.exports = roleMiddleware;
```

And apply it like this:

```
// src/routes/userRoutes.js

const express = require('express');
const { makeInvoker } = require('awilix-express');
const authMiddleware = require('../middleware/authMiddleware');
const roleMiddleware = require('../middleware/roleMiddleware');
const router = express.Router();
```

```
const userController = makeInvoker(require('../controllers/userController'));

router.get('/', authMiddleware, roleMiddleware('admin'),
userController('getAllUsers'));
router.post('/', authMiddleware, userController('createUser'));

module.exports = router;
```

Now, only those with the admin role can access the getAllUsers endpoint, no freeloaders allowed!

9.3 Error Handling and Validation

Let's face it, ah, bugs will come, it's just how it is. But we can handle them gracefully with some proper error handling, so our users don't experience a mess.

Step 1: Centralized Error Handling Middleware

Create a middleware that catches uncaught errors and gives a standard response:

```
// src/middleware/errorHandler.js

const logger = require('../logger');

const errorHandler = (err, req, res, next) => {
  logger.error(`Error: ${err.message}`);
  res.status(500).json({ error: 'Something went wrong!' });
};

module.exports = errorHandler;
```

Step 2: Applying Error Handling

Add this middleware as the last line of defence in our index.js:

```
// src/index.js

const express = require('express');
const errorHandler = require('./middleware/errorHandler');
```

85

```
// other imports...

const app = express();
// other setup...

app.use(errorHandler);

app.listen(port, () => {
  console.log(`Server running on port ${port}`);
});
```

Now, any unhandled errors will be caught here, and users get a consistent 500 Internal Server Error.

Step 3: Request Validation with Joi

Validation keeps our inputs in check, like making sure the laksa isn't too spicy! Let's make a reusable validation middleware using **Joi**:

```
// src/middleware/validate.js

const validate = (schema) => {
  return (req, res, next) => {
    const { error } = schema.validate(req.body);
    if (error) {
      return res.status(400).json({ error: error.details[0].message });
    }
    next();
  };
};
```

```
module.exports = validate;
```

And apply it to routes:

```
// src/routes/userRoutes.js

const Joi = require('joi');
```

```
// other imports...

const userSchema = Joi.object({
  name: Joi.string().min(3).required(),
  email: Joi.string().email().required(),
  password: Joi.string().min(6).required(),
  age: Joi.number().min(18).optional(),
});

router.post('/', authMiddleware, validate(userSchema), userController('createUser'));
```

This ensures all data meets our standards before being processed, keeping our app clean and safe.

Conclusion

We levelled up our Node.js skills by tackling those critical cross-cutting concerns, covering:

1. **Logging**: Using **Winston** to track every move.

2. **Monitoring**: **Prometheus** as our app's watchful eye.

3. **Authentication and Authorisation**: Securing access with **JWT** and **role-based controls**.

4. **Error Handling**: Catching mistakes with style.

5. **Request Validation**: Using **Joi** to ensure data quality.

By integrating these concerns, we keep our app robust, secure, and maintainable. Next, we'll dive into performance optimisation, tuning our app to run smoother than an MRT ride!

CHAPTER 10
BUILDING TESTABLE NODE.JS APPLICATIONS

In this Chapter, we dive into the world of **Testable Node.js Applications**! Think of testing as your code's trusty seatbelt. You might not always notice it, but when things go south, and trust me, they will, it'll save your skin. A well-tested codebase is easier to maintain, more reliable, and way less likely to ruin our sleep at 3 AM when production decides to throw a tantrum.

In this chapter, we're covering:

1. **Test-Driven Development (TDD)**: Using TDD to guide our coding journey.

2. **Unit Testing**: Testing individual bits like use cases and entities.

3. **Integration Testing**: Checking how the different parts of our app play together.

4. **End-to-End (E2E) Testing**: Testing the whole enchilada, mimicking real-world scenarios.

5. **Mocking**: Faking dependencies to focus our tests on specific logic.

Testing isn't just for those big, serious projects. It's for anyone who wants to avoid the "Oh no, why is it broken?!" moments. 😊

10.1 Introduction to Test-Driven Development (TDD)

Okay, imagine we're building a treehouse but we just start hammering away without a plan. That's how a lot of us write code sometimes. But with **Test-Driven Development (TDD)**, we flip that script: we write tests **first**, and then we write code to make those tests pass. It's like building with a blueprint, but for software.

Here's the flow of TDD, called the **Red-Green-Refactor cycle**:

1. **Red**: Write a test that fails (because, well, we haven't written the functionality yet).

2. **Green**: Write just enough code to make that test pass.

3. **Refactor**: Clean up our code, make it look nicer and more efficient, without breaking the test.

TDD keeps us laser-focused, making sure we don't end up adding stuff we don't really need. And hey, everything we build has a clear purpose from the start.

TDD in Action: A Simple Example

Let's try a basic sum function. First, we write a test that'll fail (Red):

```
// tests/sum.test.js

const sum = require('../src/sum');

describe('sum function', () => {
  it('should return the sum of two numbers', () => {
    expect(sum(2, 3)).toBe(5);
  });
});
```

Now, let's write just enough code to make that test pass (Green):

```
// src/sum.js
function sum(a, b) {
  return a + b;
}

module.exports = sum;
```

Run the test with:

```
npm test
```

Once it passes, we can clean it up if needed, but this simple function is good as is.

10.2 Unit Testing: Isolating Your Components

Unit tests are like giving each part of our code its own spotlight, checking if it behaves the way we expect. With a clean architecture, this is easier since each part of our app is already neatly separated.

Let's take a look at some unit tests for the **UserEntity** and **UserUseCases** we've built earlier.

Step 1: Unit Testing the User Entity

We'll create a test file for our UserEntity:

```
// tests/UserEntity.test.js

const UserEntity = require('../src/entities/UserEntity');

describe('UserEntity', () => {
  it('should create a user with valid attributes', () => {
    const user = new UserEntity({
      id: '123',
      name: 'John Doe',
      email: 'john@example.com',
      age: 30,
    });

    expect(user.name).toBe('John Doe');
    expect(user.email).toBe('john@example.com');
  });

  it('should throw an error if the email format is invalid', () => {
    const user = new UserEntity({
      id: '123',
      name: 'John Doe',
      email: 'invalid-email',
      age: 30,
    });
```

```
    expect(() => user.changeEmail('invalid-email')).toThrow('Invalid email format');
  });
});
```

Step 2: Unit Testing the User Use Cases

Now, let's test the business logic in our use cases. We'll mock the repository layer so that we're only testing the logic, not the database.

```
// tests/UserUseCases.test.js

const UserUseCases = require('../src/use-cases/userUseCases');

describe('UserUseCases', () => {
  const mockRepository = {
    findById: jest.fn(),
    save: jest.fn(),
    update: jest.fn(),
    deleteById: jest.fn(),
  };

  const userUseCases = new UserUseCases(mockRepository);

  it('should create a new user', async () => {
    const userData = { name: 'John Doe', email: 'john@example.com', age: 30 };
    mockRepository.save.mockResolvedValue(userData);

    const user = await userUseCases.createUser(userData);

    expect(mockRepository.save).toHaveBeenCalled();
    expect(user.name).toBe('John Doe');
  });

  it('should update an existing user', async () => {
```

```
const user = { id: '123', name: 'John Doe', email: 'john@example.com', age: 30 };
mockRepository.findById.mockResolvedValue(user);
mockRepository.save.mockResolvedValue({ ...user, email:
'new.email@example.com' });

const updatedUser = await userUseCases.updateUserEmail('123',
'new.email@example.com');

expect(updatedUser.email).toBe('new.email@example.com');
expect(mockRepository.save).toHaveBeenCalled();
});
});
```

By mocking the repository, we focus entirely on the business logic in our use cases, leaving out database interactions for now.

10.3 Integration Testing: How Parts Work Together

Integration tests are all about checking how our app's components interact. It's like testing the connections between our use cases and repositories to ensure data flows correctly.

This time, we'll use an actual MongoDB instance, but don't worry, we won't touch production data. We'll use an in-memory database or a Docker container for testing.

Step 1: Setting Up MongoDB for Testing

Let's use **mongodb-memory-server** to run a MongoDB instance in-memory.

First, install it:

npm install mongodb-memory-server --save-dev

Now, let's write an integration test:

// tests/UserUseCases.integration.test.js

const { MongoMemoryServer } = require('mongodb-memory-server');
const mongoose = require('mongoose');
const UserModel = require('../src/models/User');

```javascript
const MongoUserRepository = require('../src/repositories/MongoUserRepository');
const UserUseCases = require('../src/use-cases/userUseCases');

let mongoServer;

describe('UserUseCases Integration Tests', () => {
  beforeAll(async () => {
    mongoServer = await MongoMemoryServer.create();
    const uri = mongoServer.getUri();

    await mongoose.connect(uri, { useNewUrlParser: true, useUnifiedTopology:
true });
  });

  afterAll(async () => {
    await mongoose.disconnect();
    await mongoServer.stop();
  });

  const userRepository = new MongoUserRepository(UserModel);
  const userUseCases = new UserUseCases(userRepository);

  it('should create and retrieve a user', async () => {
    const userData = { name: 'John Doe', email: 'john@example.com', age: 30 };
    const newUser = await userUseCases.createUser(userData);

    expect(newUser.name).toBe('John Doe');

    const retrievedUser = await userUseCases.getUserById(newUser._id);
    expect(retrievedUser.email).toBe('john@example.com');
  });

  it('should update an existing user', async () => {
```

```
  const userData = { name: 'Jane Doe', email: 'jane@example.com', age: 25 };
  const newUser = await userUseCases.createUser(userData);

  const updatedUser = await userUseCases.updateUserEmail(newUser._id,
'new.email@example.com');
  expect(updatedUser.email).toBe('new.email@example.com');
 });
});
```

Step 2: Running Integration Tests

Run the tests with:

npm test

Now, we're testing real interactions between our MongoDB and the app, ensuring the data flows as expected.

10.4 End-to-End (E2E) Testing: Testing the Whole System

End-to-End (E2E) tests simulate how users interact with our app. This tests our entire stack, from HTTP requests all the way down to the database.

Step 1: Setting Up Supertest

First, install **Supertest**:

npm install supertest --save-dev

Step 2: Writing an E2E Test

Let's create an E2E test for our user routes:

// tests/userRoutes.e2e.test.js

```
const request = require('supertest');
const app = require('../src/index');
const { MongoMemoryServer } = require('mongodb-memory-server');
const mongoose = require('mongoose');

let mongoServer;
```

```
beforeAll(async () => {
  mongoServer = await MongoMemoryServer.create();
  const uri = mongoServer.getUri();

  await mongoose.connect(uri, { use

NewUrlParser: true, useUnifiedTopology: true });
});

afterAll(async () => {
  await mongoose.disconnect();
  await mongoServer.stop();
});

describe('User Routes E2E', () => {
  it('should create and retrieve a user', async () => {
    const userData = { name: 'John Doe', email: 'john@example.com', password:
'password123', age: 30 };

    const createResponse = await request(app).post('/users').send(userData);
    expect(createResponse.status).toBe(201);
    expect(createResponse.body.data.name).toBe('John Doe');

    const getResponse = await request(app).get(`/users/$
{createResponse.body.data._id}`);
    expect(getResponse.status).toBe(200);
    expect(getResponse.body.data.email).toBe('john@example.com');
  });

  it('should update a user email', async () => {
    const userData = { name: 'Jane Doe', email: 'jane@example.com', password:
'password123', age: 25 };
```

```
const createResponse = await request(app).post('/users').send(userData);

const updateResponse = await request(app)
  .put(`/users/${createResponse.body.data._id}/email`)
  .send({ email: 'new.email@example.com' });

expect(updateResponse.status).toBe(200);
expect(updateResponse.body.data.email).toBe('new.email@example.com');
});
});
```

Step 3: Running E2E Tests

Run this with:

npm test

Now, our E2E test ensures that the whole system, from HTTP requests through to the database, behaves correctly.

10.5 Mocking Dependencies for Isolation

Sometimes, we need to test one part of our app without worrying about the rest. That's where **mocking** comes in, creating "fake" versions of dependencies so we can focus on testing specific logic.

Let's mock a database call in a controller test:

```
// tests/userController.test.js

const { createUser } = require('../src/controllers/userController')({
  userUseCases: {
    createUser: jest.fn().mockResolvedValue({ id: '123', name: 'John Doe' }),
  },
});

describe('UserController', () => {
  it('should create a new user', async () => {
```

```
  const req = { body: { name: 'John Doe', email: 'john@example.com', password:
'password123' } };
  const res = {
   status: jest.fn().mockReturnThis(),
   json: jest.fn(),
  };

  await createUser(req, res);

  expect(res.status).toHaveBeenCalledWith(201);
  expect(res.json).toHaveBeenCalledWith({ data: { id: '123', name: 'John Doe' } });
 });
});
```

By mocking userUseCases.createUser, we ensure our tests are quick and isolated, without relying on external systems.

Conclusion

We've made our Node.js applications **testable** by diving into unit, integration, and end-to-end tests. Here's what we've covered:

1. **Test-Driven Development (TDD)**: Using tests to guide our development.

2. **Unit Testing**: Testing components like entities and use cases individually.

3. **Integration Testing**: Checking if different layers work well together.

4. **End-to-End Testing (E2E)**: Testing real-world interactions across the whole system.

5. **Mocking**: Creating fake dependencies to keep our tests focused and efficient.

Testing is our safety net, keeping our app solid as we build and expand. As we move on to the next chapter, we'll tackle performance optimization, scaling, and caching in Node.js to ensure our app can handle the wild world of production.

CHAPTER 11
IMPLEMENTING EVENT-DRIVEN ARCHITECTURE (EDA) – FOR OUR FELLOW DEVELOPERS

In this Chapter, we're diving into the exciting world of **Event-Driven Architecture (EDA)**. Think of EDA as turning our Node.js app into a **super-social extrovert**, the kind that loves to react to things, broadcast messages, and keep the conversation flowing between different parts of our system. With EDA, our app gets a personality: it's reactive, scalable, and modular.

In this chapter, we're going to:

1. Get a solid understanding of **Event-Driven Architecture**.

2. Break down **CQRS (Command Query Responsibility Segregation)** and **Event Sourcing**.

3. Build some **Event Handlers** and **Dispatchers** in Node.js.

4. Hook up **MongoDB** with event streams using Change Streams.

5. Get cozy with **Kafka, RabbitMQ, or Redis** for asynchronous event processing.

We'll be transforming our app into a vibrant event-driven party, so let's lace up our coding shoes and get dancing with some events!

11.1 Introduction to Event-Driven Architecture

What is Event-Driven Architecture?

Event-Driven Architecture (EDA) is like the kopitiam (coffee shop) of software architecture. It's all about reacting to what's happening around us. Here, the flow of our app is determined by **events**. Imagine a user signs up, adds a product to their cart, or places an order, each of these actions triggers a response somewhere in our app.

Rather than tightly coupling components together (like that friend who always jio others out but never shows up), EDA uses **event emitters** and **event listeners**. So, components communicate by shooting off **events** and listening for them without needing to know each other's business. It keeps our code clean, flexible, and scalable.

Key Components in EDA

1. **Events**: These are like announcements saying something happened (e.g., "A new user signed up!"). **Producers**: The folks who shout out the events.

2. **Consumers**: The ones who listen and react to those events.

3. **Event Bus**: The postman (like RabbitMQ, Kafka, or Redis) that delivers messages from producers to consumers.

Real-World Analogy:

Picture a hawker centre with a fire alarm system. If a fire breaks out (the **event**), the alarm system (the **producer**) sends out alerts. Firefighters (the **consumers**) respond and extinguish the flames. The alarm doesn't care which fire station hears the alert, and the firefighters don't worry about where the alarm came from, they just do their job. This decoupling is what makes EDA so flexible!

Benefits of Event-Driven Architecture

1. **Loose Coupling**: Components don't need to know each other's details, making our lives easier when we want to change or replace things.

2. **Scalability**: We can scale different parts independently, like adding more hawkers to a busy food court.

3. **Real-Time Reactions**: Perfect for real-time needs like sending notifications, processing payments, or monitoring stock levels.

11.2 CQRS and Event Sourcing Principles

Before we jump into the code, let's touch on two crucial concepts that pair well with EDA: **CQRS** and **Event Sourcing**.

CQRS (Command Query Responsibility Segregation)

CQRS separates the responsibilities of **reading** (queries) from **writing** (commands). It's like having one chef for frying eggs and another for brewing coffee. The system that handles reading data is different from the one that changes data.

- **Commands**: These are actions that change the state (e.g., "Add laksa to order").

- **Queries**: These just fetch data (e.g., "How many laksas were sold?").

In an EDA setup, commands often kick off events, while queries simply ask about the current state.

Event Sourcing

Event Sourcing is all about storing the history of what happened rather than just the latest state. Instead of just storing that an order was delivered, we store each step that got us there (e.g., "Order Placed," "Order Shipped," "Order Delivered"). Replaying these events gives us the current state. It's like rewinding the CCTV footage to see how we ended up with that last bowl of laksa.

11.3 Implementing Event Handlers and Dispatchers in Node.js

Let's roll up our sleeves and get hands-on with some code! We'll build a simple event-driven system using Node.js. Here's our plan: we'll make an **event dispatcher** using Node's EventEmitter so that different parts of our app can chit-chat by emitting and listening for events.

Step 1: Creating an Event Dispatcher

Let's set up our event bus using Node.js's built-in EventEmitter module.

```
// src/eventBus.js

const EventEmitter = require('events');

class EventBus extends EventEmitter {}
```

```
const eventBus = new EventBus();

module.exports = eventBus;
```

Step 2: Emitting and Listening for Events

Let's set up a scenario: when a user signs up, we'll emit an event that triggers sending a welcome email.

1. **UserService**: Handles creating a user and emitting an event after creation.

2. **EmailService**: Listens for UserCreated events to send a welcome email.

UserService: Emitting an Event

```
// src/services/UserService.js
const eventBus = require('../eventBus');

class UserService {
  createUser(userData) {
    // Simulate saving the user to the database
    const user = { id: Date.now(), ...userData };

    console.log('User created:', user);

    // Emit a 'UserCreated' event
    eventBus.emit('UserCreated', user);
    return user;
  }
}

module.exports = new UserService();
```

EmailService: Listening for an Event

```
// src/services/EmailService.js
const eventBus = require('../eventBus');
```

```javascript
class EmailService {
  constructor() {
    // Listen for 'UserCreated' events
    eventBus.on('UserCreated', this.sendWelcomeEmail);
  }

  sendWelcomeEmail(user) {
    console.log(`Sending welcome email to ${user.email}`);
    // Simulate sending an email
  }
}

module.exports = new EmailService();
```

Step 3: Putting It All Together

Now, let's create a controller that handles user registration.

```javascript
// src/controllers/userController.js

const UserService = require('../services/UserService');

const createUser = (req, res) => {
  const user = UserService.createUser(req.body);
  res.status(201).json({ data: user });
};

module.exports = { createUser };
```

Step 4: Testing the Event-Driven Flow

Let's add a route to test this flow.

```javascript
// src/routes/userRoutes.js

const express = require('express');
const router = express.Router();
const { createUser } = require('../controllers/userController');
```

```
router.post('/', createUser);

module.exports = router;
```

Step 5: Testing Our Setup

Start our app and send a POST request to create a user:

```
curl -X POST http://localhost:3000/users -H "Content-Type: application/json" -d
'{"name": "Ah Beng", "email": "ahbeng@example.com"}'
```

Expected output:

```
User created: { id: 1635524359034, name: 'Ah Beng', email:
'ahbeng@example.com' }
```

Sending welcome email to ahbeng@example.com

Here, the UserCreated event is emitted, and the EmailService listens for it to send a welcome email. Solid, right?

11.4 Integrating MongoDB with Event Streams

MongoDB's **Change Streams** let us listen for changes in collections (like new inserts) and react to them, great for real-time apps.

Step 1: Setting Up MongoDB Change Streams

Let's build a change stream that watches for new users.

```
// src/services/MongoChangeStreamService.js

const mongoose = require('mongoose');
const eventBus = require('../eventBus');

const UserModel = require('../models/User');

class MongoChangeStreamService {
  constructor() {
    // Start watching the User collection for changes
    this.changeStream = UserModel.watch();
```

103

```javascript
    // Listen for insert events
    this.changeStream.on('change', (change) => {
      if (change.operationType === 'insert') {
        const user = change.fullDocument;
        console.log('New user detected in MongoDB:', user);

        // Emit an event for the new user
        eventBus.emit('UserCreatedInMongo', user);
      }
    });
  }
}

module.exports = new MongoChangeStreamService();
```

Step 2: Reacting to MongoDB Events

Update our EmailService to listen for these MongoDB-based events.

```javascript
// src/services/EmailService.js

const eventBus = require('../eventBus');

class EmailService {
  constructor() {
    eventBus.on('UserCreatedInMongo', this.sendWelcomeEmail);
  }

  sendWelcomeEmail(user) {
    console.log(`Sending welcome email to ${user.email}`);
  }
}

module.exports = new EmailService();
```

Now, when a user is inserted into MongoDB, the change stream will catch it, and our email service will react like a pro.

11.5 Event Processing with Kafka, RabbitMQ, or Redis

For large-scale systems, sometimes our events need to travel across services. Enter **Kafka**, **RabbitMQ**, and **Redis Pub/Sub**, our event messengers.

Step 1: Setting Up Redis

First, install the **ioredis** package:

npm install ioredis

Step 2: Creating Redis Event Publisher

Let's make a service that publishes events to a Redis channel.

```
// src/services/RedisPublisher.js

const Redis = require('ioredis');
const redis = new Redis();

class RedisPublisher {
  publishUserCreated(user) {
    redis.publish('UserCreatedChannel', JSON.stringify(user));
  }
}

module.exports = new RedisPublisher();
```

Step 3: Creating Redis Event Subscriber

Now, let's make a subscriber to listen for those events.

```
// src/services/RedisSubscriber.js

const Redis = require('ioredis');
const redis = new Redis();
const eventBus = require('../eventBus');
```

```
class RedisSubscriber {
  constructor() {
    redis.subscribe('UserCreatedChannel', () => {
      console.log('Subscribed to UserCreatedChannel');
    });

    redis.on('message', (channel, message) => {
      if (channel === 'UserCreatedChannel') {
        const user = JSON.parse(message);
        console.log('Received user created event:', user);

        // Emit locally
        eventBus.emit('UserCreatedInRedis', user);
      }
    });
  }
}

module.exports = new RedisSubscriber();
```

Step 4: Reacting to Redis Events

Update our EmailService again to react to Redis events.

```
// src/services/EmailService.js

const eventBus = require('../eventBus');

class EmailService {
  constructor() {
    eventBus.on('UserCreatedInRedis', this.sendWelcomeEmail);
  }

  sendWelcomeEmail(user) {
    console.log(`Sending welcome email to ${user.email}`);
  }
```

```
}

module.exports = new EmailService();
```

With this setup, our **UserService** publishes events to Redis, and **RedisSubscriber** picks them up, allowing **EmailService** to send a welcome email. Easy peasy.

Summary

In this chapter, we dived deep into **Event-Driven Architecture (EDA)** and saw how it turns our Node.js app into a responsive and scalable setup. Here's a quick recap:

1. Mastered the fundamentals of **EDA**, making our code more maintainable and scalable.

2. Explored **CQRS** and **Event Sourcing**, and their synergy with EDA.

3. Built a simple event bus using **Node.js's EventEmitter**.

4. Used **MongoDB Change Streams** for real-time reactions to database changes.

5. Learned to process events asynchronously with **Redis Pub/Sub**.

CHAPTER 12
PERFORMANCE OPTIMIZATION IN CLEAN ARCHITECTURE

In this Chapter, We're diving into making our Node.js and MongoDB applications zippier than a hawker stall auntie dishing out satay at peak hour. This chapter's all about squeezing every bit of speed and efficiency out of our apps, whether it's through fine-tuning the inner workings of Node.js, streamlining how Express manages requests, supercharging our MongoDB queries, or adding a dash of **caching** magic with Redis. Plus, we'll touch on **data partitioning** and **sharding** to manage our data as it scales. Ready? Let's get going!

12.1 Optimizing Node.js for High-Performance Applications

Node.js runs on the **V8 JavaScript engine** (the same engine that powers Google Chrome), so it's already pretty fast. But like a souped-up race car, it needs the right adjustments to really fly. Understanding the **event loop** and **asynchronous programming** is where we unlock that extra power. So let's dig into how we can make Node.js sing.

Event Loop, Asynchronous Programming, and Promises

The Node.js **event loop** is the secret sauce behind its non-blocking nature. It's what allows our apps to handle tons of requests without choking. Think of it like a coffee stall uncle who's always taking orders while brewing coffee, it's all about multitasking!

The Event Loop: A Quick Refresher

Everything in Node.js revolves around the **event loop**. Unlike traditional servers that block while waiting for tasks like database queries, Node.js keeps things moving:

1. **Incoming events** (e.g., HTTP requests) are added to the event queue.

2. When an event is ready, its **callback** is sent to the call stack.

3. The event loop keeps processing callbacks one by one, never sitting idle.

Imagine our app as a busy kopitiam (coffee shop) with Node.js as the uncle taking orders. He doesn't wait around for the food to be ready before taking the next order, he just moves on and comes back when it's done.

Code Example: Non-blocking I/O

Here's a quick example to show how Node.js handles things without blocking:

```
const fs = require('fs');

console.log('Start reading file...');
fs.readFile('example.txt', 'utf8', (err, data) => {
  if (err) {
    console.error('Error reading file', err);
    return;
  }
  console.log('File content:', data);
});
console.log('Reading file initiated...');
```

Output:

Start reading file...

Reading file initiated...

File content: Hello, Node.js!

Notice how Reading file initiated... appears before the file content? That's the event loop continuing with other work while the file reads in the background, just like the coffee uncle serving another customer while waiting for the coffee to brew.`**Promises and async/await for Asynchronous Programming**

We all want our code to be easy to read, right? That's where **Promises** and async/await come in. They allow us to write asynchronous code that *looks* like synchronous code, making our lives a whole lot easier.

Code Example: async/await

```
const fs = require('fs').promises;
async function readFileAsync() {
  try {
    const data = await fs.readFile('example.txt', 'utf8');
    console.log('File content:', data);
  } catch (err) {
    console.error('Error reading file', err);
  }
}


readFileAsync();
```

Same result, but way cleaner, right? No more messy callbacks! This is especially handy when our app scales up, and we need to handle more complex workflows.

Optimising Express.js Middlewares and Route Handling

If our Node.js app is using **Express**, we need to be smart about how we handle middleware. Middleware functions are like security guards at a club, they check each incoming request before it goes inside. But too many guards, and there'll be a bottleneck at the entrance.

1. Use Asynchronous Handlers

If our middleware or routes are doing heavy lifting (like querying a database), make them async so the event loop can keep working on other requests. Here's an example:

```
app.get('/users', async (req, res) => {
  try {
    const users = await getUsersFromDatabase();
    res.json(users);
  } catch (err) {
    res.status(500).json({ error: err.message });
```

```
}
});
```

2. Limit the Use of Global Middlewares

Apply middleware only where it's needed. For instance, we might not need logging for a simple health check endpoint:

```
// Apply logging middleware only to user routes

app.use('/users', loggerMiddleware);
```

3. Implement Caching with Redis

Why keep fetching the same data from our database when we can cache it with Redis? Think of Redis as our "regular customer" memory, once we've served them, we remember their order.

```
const redisClient = require('./redisClient'); // Assume Redis is already set up

app.get('/users/:id', async (req, res) => {
  const userId = req.params.id;

  const cachedUser = await redisClient.get(userId);
  if (cachedUser) {
    return res.json(JSON.parse(cachedUser));
  }

  const user = await getUserFromDatabase(userId);
  redisClient.setex(userId, 3600, JSON.stringify(user)); // Cache for 1 hour

  res.json(user);
});
```

This way, if someone asks for the same user info, Redis answers directly without bothering the database.

12.2 MongoDB Performance Tuning

MongoDB is like a super-organised data library, but we need to know how to use the Dewey Decimal System (or its equivalent) to get the most out of it. Here, we'll look at **indexing**, **query optimisation**, and more caching tricks.

Indexing Strategies and Query Optimisation

Indexes in MongoDB are like bookmarks in a thick book, they let us find specific pages without flipping through every single one. Let's get our queries speeding along!

Creating Indexes

If our queries often search on fields like email or createdAt, creating indexes on those fields is a game-changer:

```
// Create an index on the 'email' field

db.users.createIndex({ email: 1 });
```

With this, MongoDB can quickly find users by email without scanning the whole collection.

Compound Indexes

Got queries with multiple conditions? **Compound indexes** have our back:

```
// Create a compound index on 'createdAt' and 'email'

db.users.createIndex({ createdAt: 1, email: 1 });
```

Now, queries like "Get users created after X date and sort by email" will be super snappy.

Query Optimization with explain()

Want to see how MongoDB handles a query under the hood? Use explain():

```
db.users.find({ email:'john@example.com' }).explain('executionStats');
```

This gives us the lowdown on whether MongoDB is using our index or wasting time scanning the whole collection.

Caching Strategies with Redis

Just like earlier, Redis can help reduce the load on MongoDB by caching frequent queries. Here's an example:

```
const redis = require('redis');
const redisClient = redis.createClient();

async function getCachedUser(userId) {
 const cachedUser = await redisClient.getAsync(userId);
 if (cachedUser) {
   return JSON.parse(cachedUser);
 }

 const user = await UserModel.findById(userId);
 redisClient.setex(userId, 3600, JSON.stringify(user)); // Cache for 1 hour
 return user;
}
```

Avoiding N+1 Query Problems

The **N+1 problem** is like ordering satay one stick at a time instead of a whole plate, it's super inefficient. We can solve this with **MongoDB aggregation** or **populate** queries to fetch related documents all at once:

```
const usersWithPosts = await UserModel.find().populate('posts');
```

Now we get the users *and* their posts in a single go, no more back-and-forth!

12.3 Using Data Partitioning and Sharding with MongoDB

Handling massive datasets? Single servers won't cut it. It's time to think big with **sharding**.

What is Sharding?

Sharding is splitting our database into smaller pieces across multiple servers. Think of it as dividing our mee rebus order between multiple stalls to serve everyone faster.

How Sharding Works

1. **Shards**: Each shard is a replica set that holds a portion of our data.

2. **Config Servers**: Store metadata and configurations for the cluster.

3. **Mongos Router**: Routes queries to the correct shard.

With sharding, we can handle way more data without slowing down. Perfect for scaling up when our user base grows!

Summary

We'll have our Node.js and MongoDB apps running like a well-oiled MRT train, no delays, no hiccups, just smooth operations. Ready to put the pedal to the metal? Let's optimize!

CHAPTER 13
DEPLOYING NODE.JS APPLICATIONS

In this Chapter, we're getting hands-on with **Deploying Node.js Applications**! Think of it like prepping for a big durian feast, getting everything just right so it's a treat (and not a disaster) when we finally share it with the world. We've built the app (our "durian"), now it's time to make sure it's ready for the world to enjoy. Once we go live, there's no turning back, so we need to be prepared, secure, and scalable, lah!

In this chapter, we'll cover:

1. **Preparing for Production Deployment**: Making sure our Node.js app is secure and ready for the wild.

2. **Continuous Integration and Continuous Deployment (CI/CD)**: Setting up automated pipelines to make deployments smooth like kaya toast.

3. **Dockerizing Your Application**: Wrapping up our Node.js app with Docker to make it easy to run on the cloud.

Let's get our Node.js app all geared up for production, ready to handle whatever comes its way!

13.1 Preparing for Production Deployment

Deploying a Node.js application isn't as simple as kopi-o kosong (a black coffee). It's more like kopi siu dai (coffee with less sugar), we've got to adjust things just right to get the perfect blend. To ensure that our app behaves properly in the production, we have to manage configurations, secure our app, and handle processes like an expert.

Environment Configuration and Security Considerations

Our app needs to adapt to different environments: development, testing, and production. That means we've got to handle environment variables and configurations properly so it doesn't act up when it's live. Let's dive into how to manage this.

1. Environment Variables

We'll store sensitive information like API keys and database credentials in a .env file. This way, our secrets stay hidden and our app can switch settings smoothly across environments.

1.   Install the dotenv library, which loads environment variables from the .env file:

npm install dotenv

1.   Create a .env file at the root of our project:

PORT=3000

MONGO_URI=mongodb://localhost:27017/myapp

JWT_SECRET=super_secret_key

2.   In server.js, load environment variables like this:

```
require('dotenv').config();
const express = require('express');
const mongoose = require('mongoose');

const app = express();
const port = process.env.PORT || 3000;

mongoose.connect(process.env.MONGO_URI, { useNewUrlParser: true,
useUnifiedTopology: true })
  .then(() => console.log('MongoDB connected'))
  .catch(err => console.error(err));

app.listen(port, () => {
  console.log(`Server running on port ${port}`);
});
```

With this setup, we keep sensitive info out of our codebase, making things safer and easier to manage.

2. Security Hardening

We don't want our app to kena (get hit by) security issues, so let's secure it like a HDB flat with all the locks! Here are some key steps:

- **Use HTTPS**: Encrypt all communication with SSL/TLS to keep the bad guys out.

- **Secure Headers**: Use the **helmet** library to add security headers.

npm install helmet

In server.js, add:

```
const helmet = require('helmet');

app.use(helmet());
```

- **Sanitize Inputs**: Prevent attacks like **NoSQL injection** and **XSS** by validating user inputs with libraries like **express-validator**.

npm install express-validator

Use it in our routes:

```
const { check, validationResult } = require('express-validator');
app.post('/users', [
  check('email').isEmail(),
  check('password').isLength({ min: 6 })
], (req, res) => {
  const errors = validationResult(req);
  if (!errors.isEmpty()) {
    return res.status(400).json({ errors: errors.array() });
  }
  // Continue with user creation
});
```

Using PM2 for Node.js Process Management

Once our app is live, we've got to keep it running smoothly. Think of **PM2** like a hawker uncle, it keeps an eye on things, restarts the app if it crashes, and helps us make the most of our server's CPU power.

1. **Install PM2 globally:**

npm install pm2 -g

2. **Start our app with PM2:**

pm2 start server.js --name "myapp"

3. **For multi-core magic, use the cluster mode:**

pm2 start server.js -i max --name "myapp-cluster"

This spreads the load across all CPU cores, giving our app the power to handle more requests.

4. **Monitoring with PM2**:

Monitor our app's performance and logs in real-time:

pm2 monit

5. **Make PM2 persist across reboots**:

Ensure PM2 keeps our app running, even after the server restarts:

pm2 startup

pm2 save

13.2 Continuous Integration and Continuous Deployment (CI/CD)

CI/CD is like having an auto-pilot for our deployments, running tests, building the app, and pushing it live without us lifting a finger. Let's set up a simple pipeline using **GitHub Actions**. The same idea applies if we want to use **Jenkins** or **CircleCI**.

Setting Up Pipelines (GitHub Actions, Jenkins, CircleCI)

Step 1: Create a GitHub Actions Workflow

Create a .github/workflows/ci.yml file in our repo:

name: Node.js CI

```yaml
on:
 push:
  branches: [ main ]
 pull_request:
  branches: [ main ]

jobs:
 build:
  runs-on: ubuntu-latest

  strategy:
   matrix:
    node-version: [14.x, 16.x]

  steps:
  - uses: actions/checkout@v2
  - name: Use Node.js ${{ matrix.node-version }}
   uses: actions/setup-node@v2
   with:
    node-version: ${{ matrix.node-version }}
  - run: npm install
  - run: npm test
```

This script triggers every time we push or create a pull request on main, running our tests on different Node.js versions.

Step 2: Automating Tests and Linting

To keep our code clean, let's add **ESLint**:

```
npm install eslint --save-dev
```

Add a .eslintrc.json:

```json
{
 "env": {
  "node": true,
```

```
  "es2021": true
},
"extends": "eslint:recommended",
"parserOptions": {
 "ecmaVersion": 12
},
"rules": {
 "no-console": "off"
}
}
```

Update the workflow to include linting:

- run: npm run lint

And add this script to package.json:

```
"scripts": {
 "lint": "eslint ."
}
```

Now our pipeline will ensure the code is clean before it hits production!

13.3 Dockerizing Node.js and MongoDB Applications

With **Docker**, we package our app in a nice little container, like a bento box, with everything neatly organized. This ensures that whether we run it on our machine or in the cloud, it behaves the same.

Building Docker Containers and Docker Compose for Local Development

Step 1: Creating a Dockerfile

Create a Dockerfile:

FROM node:14

WORKDIR /usr/src/app

COPY package*.json ./

RUN npm install

COPY . .

```
EXPOSE 3000

CMD ["npm", "start"]
```

Step 2: Creating a Docker Compose File

Define our services in a docker-compose.yml file:

```
version: '3'
services:
  app:
    build: .
    ports:
      - "3000:3000"
    environment:
      - MONGO_URI=mongodb://mongo:27017/myapp
    depends_on:
      - mongo

  mongo:
    image: mongo:4.4
    ports:
      - "27017:27017"
    volumes:
      - mongo-data:/data/db

volumes:
  mongo-data:
```

This setup defines a **Node.js** service and a **MongoDB** service.

Step 3: Running Your Containers

To start both containers, run:

docker-compose up --build

Now, we have our app and MongoDB running in their own containers, but they can talk to each other through Docker Compose. Shiok (awesome)!

Deploying on Cloud Platforms (AWS, Google Cloud, Heroku)

Once Docker is set up, deploying to the cloud is like a walk in the park. Let's use **AWS Elastic Beanstalk** as an example.

Step 1: Deploying to AWS Elastic Beanstalk

1. Install the **Elastic Beanstalk CLI**:

brew install aws-elasticbeanstalk

2. Initialize the project:

eb init

3. Deploy:

eb create my-node-env

eb deploy

Elastic Beanstalk will handle the heavy lifting, creating instances, setting up load balancing, and getting our app live.

Step 2: Monitoring and Scaling in AWS

AWS helps us manage our app's health and automatically scales as needed. We can tweak auto-scaling settings to add more instances during peak traffic or reduce them when things are quieter.

To monitor the app:

eb status

eb health

Set up **Amazon CloudWatch** for more insights on CPU, memory, and request metrics.

Summary

We explored key concepts for preparing a Node.js application for production deployment. We discussed the use of environment variables, securing applications with HTTPS, and managing processes with PM2. We also covered Continuous

Integration and Continuous Deployment (CI/CD) by automating testing and deployments using GitHub Actions. Additionally, we learned how to package our Node.js and MongoDB applications in Docker containers for deployment on AWS. With these skills, our Node.js app is now well-equipped for real-world challenges.

CHAPTER 14
CASE STUDY: REAL-WORLD APPLICATION USING CLEAN ARCHITECTURE

In this chapter, we get our hands dirty and make theory come alive by building a real-world **E-Commerce Application**. But no worries, we're not just throwing code around, everything we do will follow the **Clean Architecture** principles we've been discussing throughout this book. Let's see how all those layers, **Domain, Use Cases, Repositories, and Presentation**, gel together in a real-world scenario. And, ah, we'll also explore how to **test**, **deploy**, and **monitor** this baby to make sure it's ready for production.

In this chapter, we'll:

1. Break down the **requirements** and **architecture** of a simple yet functional e-commerce project.

2. Build the **Domain Layer** that handles our core business logic.

3. Set up **Use Cases** and **Repositories** to manage application flow and data access.

4. Design **RESTful APIs** to interact with our system and process incoming requests.

5. Cover **testing**, **deployment**, and **monitoring** strategies to ensure our app is rock solid.

Sound good? Alright, let's power up our IDEs and get cracking!

14.1 Overview of a Sample E-Commerce Project

Before diving into code, let's understand what our e-commerce system will look like. We'll keep things simple, just the essentials of an e-commerce platform, like the must-haves that customers expect.

Basic Requirements:

1. **User Registration and Authentication**: Users should be able to sign up, log in, and update their profiles. This is the heart of most apps, right?

2. **Product Catalog**: Show off a list of products with details like price, description, and category.

3. **Shopping Cart**: Users should add items to their carts and manage them before making that purchase.

4. **Order Management**: Users can place orders, and our system will process them.

5. **Admin Features**: Admins need some power, right? They should be able to add or update products, manage orders, and view reports.

High-Level Architecture

We'll use **Clean Architecture** to organise our system, breaking it down into independent layers like this:

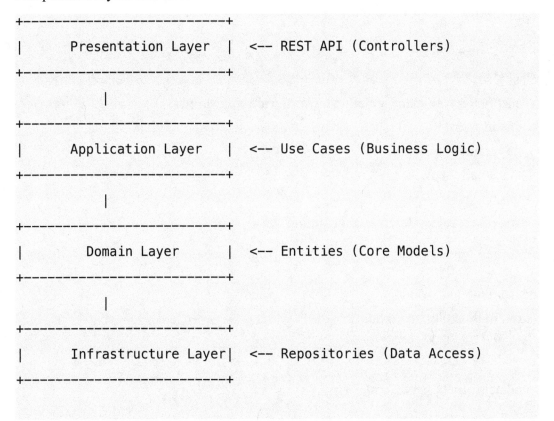

Each layer has a specific role, and they all follow the **Dependency Inversion Principle**. Higher-level layers don't depend directly on lower ones, instead, they work with abstractions (interfaces). That way, we keep our code clean and easy to maintain.

14.2 Implementing the Domain Layer for the E-Commerce Application

Now we're talking! Let's dive into the **Domain Layer**, the heart of Clean Architecture. This layer is where we define the core business logic and rules, things that are central to our app, like users, products, and orders.

Step 1: Defining Domain Entities

We'll need three main entities to start with:

1.   **User Product Order**

These entities will represent the key aspects of our business logic. Let's build them!

User Entity

```
// src/entities/User.js

class User {
  constructor({ id, name, email, password, role = 'customer' }) {
    this.id = id;
    this.name = name;
    this.email = email;
    this.password = password;
    this.role = role; // 'customer' or 'admin'
  }

  isAdmin() {
    return this.role === 'admin';
  }

  updateProfile({ name, email }) {
```

```
    this.name = name;
    this.email = email;
  }
}

module.exports = User;
```

This User entity is like a mini police, keeping user roles in check and managing profile updates.

Product Entity

```
// src/entities/Product.js
class Product {
  constructor({ id, name, description, price, category }) {
    this.id = id;
    this.name = name;
    this.description = description;
    this.price = price;
    this.category = category;
  }

  updatePrice(newPrice) {
    if (newPrice <= 0) {
      throw new Error('Price must be greater than zero.');
    }
    this.price = newPrice;
  }
}

module.exports = Product;
```

Our Product entity makes sure that prices are always positive, no freebie bugs here, haha!

Order Entity

```
// src/entities/Order.js
class Order {
  constructor({ id, userId, products = [], status = 'pending' }) {
    this.id = id;
    this.userId = userId;
    this.products = products;
    this.status = status; // 'pending', 'completed', 'shipped'
  }

  addProduct(productId, quantity) {
    this.products.push({ productId, quantity });
  }

  updateStatus(newStatus) {
    const validStatuses = ['pending', 'completed', 'shipped'];
    if (!validStatuses.includes(newStatus)) {
      throw new Error('Invalid status');
    }
    this.status = newStatus;
  }
}

module.exports = Order;
```

Here's our Order entity, which helps us keep track of the order status and manage items. It ensures the business rules of orders are properly enforced.

14.3 Developing Use Cases and Repositories

With our core entities in place, let's move on to the **Application Layer**. This is where we define **Use Cases**, the actions our application can perform.

We'll create use cases for:

1. **User Management**: Registering, logging in, and updating user profiles.

2. **Product Management**: Creating, updating, and fetching products.

3. **Order Management**: Placing orders and updating order statuses.

Step 1: Implementing Use Cases

These use cases will coordinate the interactions between entities and repositories.

User Use Cases

```
// src/use-cases/userUseCases.js

class UserUseCases {
  constructor(userRepository) {
    this.userRepository = userRepository;
  }

  async registerUser(userData) {
    const user = new User(userData);
    await this.userRepository.save(user);
    return user;
  }

  async loginUser(email, password) {
    const user = await this.userRepository.findByEmail(email);
    if (!user || user.password !== password) {
      throw new Error('Invalid credentials');
    }
    return user;
  }

  async updateUserProfile(userId, profileData) {
    const user = await this.userRepository.findById(userId);
    user.updateProfile(profileData);
    await this.userRepository.save(user);
    return user;
  }
```

```
}
```

```
module.exports = UserUseCases;
```

These use cases ensure that user actions like registration and login are handled properly.

Product Use Cases

```
// src/use-cases/productUseCases.js
class ProductUseCases {
  constructor(productRepository) {
    this.productRepository = productRepository;
  }

  async createProduct(productData) {
    const product = new Product(productData);
    await this.productRepository.save(product);
    return product;
  }

  async getProductById(productId) {
    return this.productRepository.findById(productId);
  }

  async updateProductPrice(productId, newPrice) {
    const product = await this.productRepository.findById(productId);
    product.updatePrice(newPrice);
    await this.productRepository.save(product);
    return product;
  }
}
```

```
module.exports = ProductUseCases;
```

This code handles the creation and update of product details like price changes, ensuring smooth product management.

14.4 Creating RESTful APIs and Presentation Layer

It's time to make our app talk to the outside world. The **Presentation Layer** is where we build **RESTful APIs** using **Express.js**.

Step 1: User Routes and Controllers

User Controller

```
// src/controllers/userController.js
const UserUseCases = require('../use-cases/userUseCases');
const userRepository = require('../repositories/MongoUserRepository');


const userUseCases = new UserUseCases(userRepository);


const registerUser = async (req, res) => {
  try {
    const user = await userUseCases.registerUser(req.body);
    res.status(201).json({ data: user });
  } catch (err) {
    res.status(400).json({ error: err.message });
  }
};


const loginUser = async (req, res) => {
  try {
    const user = await userUseCases.loginUser(req.body.email, req.body.password);
    res.status(200).json({ data: user });
  } catch (err) {
    res.status(400).json({ error: err.message });
  }
};
```

```
module.exports = { registerUser, loginUser };
```

These controllers make sure that incoming requests from the user routes are properly handled and passed on to the use cases.

14.5 Testing, Deployment, and Monitoring Strategies

No app is ready for prime time without testing and deployment. Let's make sure our e-commerce app is solid before shipping it out.

Step 1: Testing the E-Commerce Application

Use **Jest** and **Supertest** for writing tests that ensure our use cases and

APIs work as expected.

Step 2: Deployment Strategies

We can containerize our app using **Docker**, which makes deployment smooth across different environments. Pair this with **AWS** or **Heroku** to get it live.

Step 3: Monitoring with PM2

Use **PM2** for process management in production, and pair it with log aggregation services like **Datadog** or **Amazon CloudWatch** to keep tabs on performance and logs.

Summary

We built the order placing functionality for an **e-commerce application** using **Clean Architecture** principles. We:

1. Created the **Domain Layer** to handle the core business logic.

2. Built **Use Cases** to manage user, product, and order workflows.

3. Designed **RESTful APIs** to interact with our system.

4. Covered **testing**, **deployment**, and **monitoring** to ensure the app is production-ready.

We've covered a lot, and now, you've got the foundation to take your app from development to deployment.

CHAPTER 15
ADVANCED TOPICS AND FURTHER READING

In this Chapter, we deep dive into advanced concepts that extend the Clean Architecture principles we've been mastering. Think of this chapter as the **kueh lapis** at the end of a hearty meal, layered, rich, and packed with flavors you've yet to taste. This time, we're not just focusing on the tools like **Microservices, GraphQL APIs,** and **Domain Events,** but also on how these align with **Clean Architecture** principles. Plus, we'll introduce **Domain-Driven Design (DDD),** a crucial approach when structuring complex business logic in our applications.

Let's level up with these topics:

1. Microservices and Clean Architecture

2. GraphQL and Clean Architecture

3. Domain Events and Sagas for Complex Workflows

4. Domain-Driven Design (DDD)

5. Scaling Node.js and MongoDB Applications

These concepts are vital as our applications grow in size and complexity, helping us design software that's scalable, maintainable, and ready for real-world challenges. Let's dive in!

15.1 Microservices and Clean Architecture

What Are Microservices?

Microservices break down a large system into smaller, independently deployable services, each handling a specific domain or functionality. Think of them as stalls in a hawker centre, each focusing on a specialty, and they all come together to serve up a complete meal. Unlike a **monolithic architecture,** where everything is tightly packed into one giant app, microservices are loosely coupled and communicate over a network.

Aligning Microservices with Clean Architecture

In Clean Architecture, our goal is to separate the business logic from the technical details, things like databases, HTTP frameworks, and external APIs. By combining Clean Architecture with **microservices**, we ensure that each microservice:

- Has a well-defined **domain layer** containing core business rules.

- Uses a **use case layer** that orchestrates interactions between the domain and the outside world.

- Interacts with **infrastructure layers** for things like data persistence and messaging.

This setup makes each microservice easy to understand and modify, allowing us to iterate quickly as business needs change.

Designing a Microservice: Order and Payment Services

Let's continue with our e-commerce example:

1. **Order Service**: Handles everything related to order creation, status updates, and management.

2. **Payment Service**: Focuses on processing payments and interacting with payment gateways.

Here's a quick look at what this might look like for the **Order Service:**

```
+--------------------+
|      Entities      | <-- Core business rules (e.g., Order)
+--------------------+
|     Use Cases      | <-- Application logic (e.g., CreateOrder)
+--------------------+
| Interface Adapters | <-- REST controllers, message listeners
+--------------------+
|   Infrastructure   | <-- Database (MongoDB), messaging (RabbitMQ)
+--------------------+
```

Each service will have its own **Clean Architecture structure**, with entities, use cases, interfaces, and infrastructure.

By keeping each service's logic separated this way, our services stay clean and easy to evolve over time.

Communication Between Microservices

Microservices need to talk to each other, and we can do this either through **REST APIs** or **message brokers** (e.g., **RabbitMQ**). In Clean Architecture terms, these interactions happen through the **interface adapters**, allowing the core business logic to remain independent of communication protocols.

Example: REST-Based Communication with Clean Architecture

Here's how the **Order Service** might initiate a payment using a REST call, while keeping the logic clean:

```
// Use Case Layer: src/use-cases/InitiatePayment.js

class InitiatePayment {
 constructor(paymentService) {
  this.paymentService = paymentService;
 }

 async execute(order) {
  const paymentResult = await this.paymentService.initiatePayment(order);
  if (paymentResult.success) {
   order.markAsPaid();
  }
  return paymentResult;
 }
}

module.exports = InitiatePayment;
```

The InitiatePayment use case interacts with the paymentService, which is defined as an interface. The actual implementation of this interface could be a REST call:

```
// Interface Adapter: src/interfaces/PaymentService.js

const axios = require('axios');

class PaymentService {
  async initiatePayment(order) {
    return await axios.post('http://payment-service/pay', {
      orderId: order.id,
      amount: order.totalAmount,
    });
  }
}

module.exports = PaymentService;
```

This setup keeps the **business logic** in the use case, while the **technical details** (like REST communication) are isolated, making it easier to swap out if we decide to use a different communication method later.

15.2 Clean Architecture for GraphQL APIs

Why GraphQL?

GraphQL allows clients to request exactly the data they need, no more, no less. It's a great fit when our application serves different client types, like mobile and web apps, each requiring slightly different data.

Integrating GraphQL with Clean Architecture

With Clean Architecture, GraphQL is just another way to interact with our use cases and entities. It serves as the interface adapter between the user's requests and the application logic.

Implementing GraphQL in Clean Architecture

Here's how a GraphQL-based approach fits into the layers:

1. **Domain Layer**: Defines entities like Product and business logic.

2. **Use Case Layer**: Contains application-specific logic like CreateProduct.

3. **GraphQL Layer**: Maps GraphQL queries and mutations to use cases.

Example setup for a **Product Service**:

```
// Use Case Layer: src/use-cases/CreateProduct.js
class CreateProduct {
  constructor(productRepository) {
    this.productRepository = productRepository;
  }

  async execute(productData) {
    const product = new Product(productData);
    return await this.productRepository.save(product);
  }
}

module.exports = CreateProduct;
```

And the corresponding **GraphQL resolver**:

```
// Interface Adapter: src/graphql/resolvers/productResolver.js

const CreateProduct = require('../use-cases/CreateProduct');
const productRepository = require('../repositories/MongoProductRepository');

const createProduct = new CreateProduct(productRepository);

const resolvers = {
  Mutation: {
    createProduct: async (_, { name, price }) => {
      return await createProduct.execute({ name, price });
    }
  },
  // Other query and mutation mappings...
};

module.exports = resolvers;
```

This way, we can implement new interfaces (e.g., switching from REST to GraphQL) without having to change the core logic of our application.

15.3 Domain Events and Sagas for Complex Workflows

Domain Events

Domain Events are like messages in our application that announce when something important happens. They help keep services decoupled while still allowing them to react to each other's changes.

Implementing Domain Events in Clean Architecture

In a Clean Architecture setup, events are raised within the **domain layer** and handled through **interface adapters**:

```
// Domain Layer: src/entities/Order.js

const eventBus = require('../eventBus');

class Order {
  constructor({ id, userId, products = [], status = 'pending' }) {
    this.id = id;
    this.userId = userId;
    this.products = products;
    this.status = status;
  }

  placeOrder() {
    this.status = 'completed';
    eventBus.emit('OrderPlaced', this);
  }
}
module.exports = Order;
```

The **event bus** allows other parts of the system, like the **Payment Service**, to listen for the OrderPlaced event and act accordingly.

Sagas for Managing Long-Running Transactions

A **Saga** coordinates complex workflows that span multiple services, ensuring each part completes successfully. It can also handle **compensating transactions** to roll back actions if a failure occurs.

```javascript
// Saga Layer: src/sagas/orderSaga.js
const eventBus = require('../eventBus');

eventBus.on('OrderPlaced', async (order) => {
  try {
    await chargeCustomer(order.userId, order.totalAmount);
    await notifyShippingDepartment(order);
    await updateInventory(order);
  } catch (error) {
    console.error('Error processing order:', error);
    // Rollback actions here if needed
  }
});
```

Sagas help us maintain the integrity of workflows even when multiple services are involved, aligning with the principles of Clean Architecture by keeping the orchestration logic separate from domain-specific details.

15.4 Domain-Driven Design (DDD)

What is Domain-Driven Design?

Domain-Driven Design (DDD) is all about focusing on the **core domain**, the critical parts of the business that drive its success. It emphasises building a **ubiquitous language**, where business experts and developers speak the same language, reducing misunderstandings and aligning code closely with business needs.

Combining DDD with Clean Architecture

While Clean Architecture gives us a way to separate concerns in our codebase, DDD provides the conceptual building blocks for structuring our domain logic. Here's how they align:

- **Entities** in Clean Architecture correspond to **Aggregates** in DDD, objects that encapsulate a set of rules.

- **Use Cases** align with **Application Services** in DDD, handling operations that involve multiple aggregates.

- **Repositories** handle data persistence, working with **aggregate roots**.

Example: Applying DDD Concepts

Let's say we have an **Order** domain. Using DDD, we identify key

aggregates like Order and Payment:

```
// Domain Layer: src/entities/Order.js
class Order {
  constructor({ id, userId, products = [], status = 'pending' }) {
    this.id = id;
    this.userId = userId;
    this.products = products;
    this.status = status;
  }


  placeOrder() {
    if (this.products.length === 0) {
      throw new Error('Order must contain at least one product.');
    }
    this.status = 'completed';
    // Domain event for order placement
  }
}

module.exports = Order;
```

This Order class is an **aggregate root**, the entry point to modify an order and enforce business rules. By using DDD principles within our Clean Architecture, we ensure that our business rules are consistently enforced.

15.5 Scaling Node.js and MongoDB Applications

Scaling Node.js Horizontally

With Node.js, **horizontal scaling** means running multiple instances of our service across different servers or containers, with a load balancer distributing requests. Tools like **PM2** make it easy to manage these instances:

```
pm2 start server.js -i max  # Uses all available CPU cores
```

Scaling MongoDB with Sharding

MongoDB's **sharding** capability allows us to split large datasets across multiple servers. Sharding is crucial when our data grows beyond the capacity of a single server.

For example, to shard an orders collection based on userId:

```
# Enable sharding for a database

sh.enableSharding("ecommerce")

# Shard the orders collection by userId

sh.shardCollection("ecommerce.orders", { userId: 1 })
```

This way, each shard can handle a part of our data, allowing for scalable and highly available databases.

Summary

We explored advanced topics that integrate Clean Architecture with real-world architectural patterns:

1. **Microservices and Clean Architecture**: How to design microservices with Clean Architecture principles.

2. **GraphQL and Clean Architecture**: Integrating flexible data queries while maintaining a clean structure.

3. **Domain Events and Sagas**: Managing complex workflows and maintaining system integrity.

4. **Domain-Driven Design (DDD)**: Structuring our domain logic to reflect the core business rules.

5. **Scaling Node.js and MongoDB**: Techniques for handling more users and large data volumes.

With these concepts, our Clean Architecture-based applications are ready to scale, maintain, and adapt to evolving business requirements. This concludes our journey through Clean Architecture for Node.js and MongoDB applications, but the road ahead is full of opportunities to expand and refine these ideas.

APPENDIX

Appendix A: Node.js Best Practices for Writing Clean Code

Here we explore the best practices for writing clean, maintainable, and efficient code in **Node.js**. Think of this section as your ultimate checklist for code hygiene, it's like Marie Kondo for developers! Whether you're starting a new project or refactoring an existing one, these practices will help you keep your Node.js codebase structured, scalable, and easy to work with.

In this appendix, we'll cover:

1. Code Organisation and Modularity

2. Asynchronous Programming Best Practices

3. Error Handling and Logging

4. Security Best Practices

5. Testing Strategies for Clean Code

6. Performance Optimisation

A.1 Code Organisation and Modularity

1.1 Keep Your Files and Folders Organised

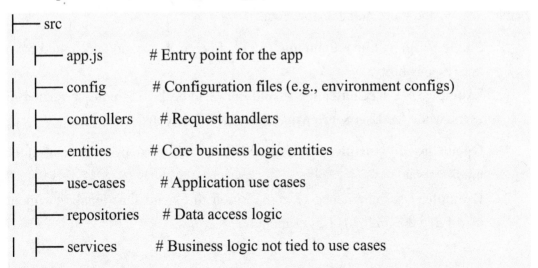

```
├── src
│   ├── app.js          # Entry point for the app
│   ├── config          # Configuration files (e.g., environment configs)
│   ├── controllers     # Request handlers
│   ├── entities        # Core business logic entities
│   ├── use-cases       # Application use cases
│   ├── repositories    # Data access logic
│   ├── services        # Business logic not tied to use cases
```

```
|   ├── routes        # Express route definitions
|   ├── middleware     # Custom middleware functions
|   └── utils         # Utility and helper functions
├── tests            # Test cases for unit, integration, and E2E tests
├── .env             # Environment variables
├── .eslintrc.json    # Linter configuration
├── package.json      # Project dependencies and scripts
└── README.md        # Documentation
```

A well-organised project structure makes it easier to navigate the codebase, collaborate with others, and scale the project over time. Above is a standard directory layout for a Node.js project following Clean Architecture principles:

Why It's Important:

- **Separation of concerns**: Each part of your application has its own well-defined responsibility.

- **Scalability**: As your application grows, it becomes easier to manage and extend with this structure.

1.2 Follow SOLID Principles

The **SOLID** principles are a set of design principles that help developers write better, cleaner, and more maintainable code.

1. **Single Responsibility Principle (SRP)**: Each class or module should have one responsibility.
   Example: A **UserController** should only handle HTTP requests related to users, while the **UserService** manages user-related business logic.

2. **Open/Closed Principle**: Classes should be open for extension but closed for modification.
   Example: Use inheritance or composition to extend functionality without modifying the original class or module.

3. **Liskov Substitution Principle**: Objects of a superclass should be replaceable with objects of a subclass without affecting the application.

4. **Interface Segregation Principle**: Don't force a class to implement interfaces it doesn't use. Split large interfaces into smaller, more specific ones.

5. **Dependency Inversion Principle (DIP)**: High-level modules should depend on abstractions, not concrete implementations.
   Example: Use interfaces (or dependency injection) to invert the dependency between use cases and repositories.

A.2 Asynchronous Programming Best Practices

2.1 Use Promises and async/await

Callbacks can lead to **callback hell**, which makes code difficult to read and maintain. Always use **Promises** or the async/await syntax to handle asynchronous code in a clean, readable way.

Example: Using Promises

```
function getDataFromDatabase() {
 return new Promise((resolve, reject) => {
  // Simulate async database call
  setTimeout(() => {
   const data = { id: 1, name: 'John Doe' };
   resolve(data);
  }, 1000);
 });
}

getDataFromDatabase()
 .then(data => console.log('Data:', data))
 .catch(error => console.error('Error:', error));
```

Example: Using async/await

```
async function fetchUser() {
```

```
try {
  const data = await getDataFromDatabase();
  console.log('Data:', data);
} catch (error) {
  console.error('Error:', error);
  }
}
```

```
fetchUser();
```

2.2 Avoid Blocking the Event Loop

The Node.js event loop is single-threaded, which means any blocking operation (e.g., CPU-intensive calculations) will prevent the event loop from processing other tasks. Offload heavy tasks to **worker threads** or use asynchronous libraries whenever possible.

Example: CPU-Intensive Blocking

```
// Blocking code
function calculateFibonacci(n) {
  if (n <= 1) return n;
  return calculateFibonacci(n - 1) + calculateFibonacci(n - 2);
}
```
For such tasks, consider using worker threads to offload the heavy lifting:
```
const { Worker } = require('worker_threads');

function runFibonacciWorker(n) {
  return new Promise((resolve, reject) => {
    const worker = new Worker('./fibonacciWorker.js', { workerData: n });
    worker.on('message', resolve);
    worker.on('error', reject);
  });
}
runFibonacciWorker(40).then(result => console.log('Fibonacci result:', result));
```

A.3 Error Handling and Logging

3.1 Centralize Error Handling with Middleware

Errors should be handled gracefully, and error handling should be centralized using **middleware** in Express. This ensures a consistent response format and prevents errors from propagating unchecked.

Example: Error Handling Middleware

```
// src/middleware/errorHandler.js

function errorHandler(err, req, res, next) {
  console.error(err.stack);
  res.status(500).json({ message: 'Internal Server Error' });
}
module.exports = errorHandler;
```

Attach the middleware to your Express app:

```
const errorHandler = require('./middleware/errorHandler');
app.use(errorHandler);
```

3.2 Use Structured Logging

Logging helps track application behavior and troubleshoot issues in production. Use structured logging libraries like **Winston** to ensure logs are consistent and easy to parse.

Example: Winston Logging

```
const { createLogger, format, transports } = require('winston');
const logger = createLogger({
  format: format.combine(
    format.timestamp(),
    format.json()
  ),
  transports: [new transports.Console(), new transports.File({ filename: 'app.log' })]
});

logger.info('Application started');
```

A.4 Security Best Practices

4.1 Sanitize User Input

Always validate and sanitize user inputs to prevent **SQL Injection**, **NoSQL Injection**, and **Cross-Site Scripting (XSS)** attacks.

Example: Using express-validator for Input Validation

```
const { check, validationResult } = require('express-validator');
app.post('/register', [
  check('email').isEmail(),
  check('password').isLength({ min: 6 })
], (req, res) => {
  const errors = validationResult(req);
  if (!errors.isEmpty()) {
    return res.status(400).json({ errors: errors.array() });
  }
  // Proceed with user registration
});
```

4.2 Use HTTPS in Production

Always serve your application over **HTTPS** in production to encrypt data between the client and the server. Tools like **Let's Encrypt** can provide free SSL certificates.

4.3 Use Environment Variables for Sensitive Data

Never hardcode sensitive information (like API keys or database credentials) in your source code. Use environment variables and the dotenv library to manage them securely.

```
# .env file
```

```
DATABASE_URL=mongodb://localhost:27017/myapp
```

```
JWT_SECRET=supersecretkey
```

Load these variables at runtime:

```
require('dotenv').config();
```

```
const jwtSecret = process.env.JWT_SECRET;
```

A.5 Testing Strategies for Clean Code

5.1 Write Unit Tests for Business Logic

Focus on writing **unit tests** for your business logic, especially in the domain and use case layers. Use **Jest** for testing, and isolate external dependencies by mocking them.

Example: Testing a Use Case

```
const UserUseCases = require('../src/use-cases/userUseCases');

describe('UserUseCases', () => {

  const mockUserRepository = {

    save: jest.fn(),

    findByEmail: jest.fn(),

  };

  const userUseCases = new UserUseCases(mockUserRepository);


  it('should register a new user', async () => {

    const userData = { name: 'John Doe', email: 'john@example.com',
password: 'password' };

    const newUser = await userUseCases.registerUser(userData);


expect(mockUserRepository.save).toHaveBeenCalledWith(expect.objectCon
taining(userData));

    expect(newUser.name).toBe('John Doe');

  });

});
```

5.2 Use Integration and E2E Tests

Integration tests verify how different components of your system work together (e.g., testing controllers and repositories). **End-to-end (E2E) tests** simulate real-world usage of your application by testing the entire flow from a user's perspective.

Use **Supertest** for integration testing:

```
const request = require

('supertest');
const app = require('../src/app');

describe('User Routes', () => {
  it('should register a new user via API', async () => {
    const response = await request(app)
      .post('/users/register')
      .send({ name: 'John', email: 'john@example.com', password: 'password' });

    expect(response.status).toBe(201);
    expect(response.body.data.name).toBe('John');
  });
});
```

A.6 Performance Optimization

6.1 Cache Expensive Operations with Redis

For expensive operations (like database queries or API calls), use **Redis** to cache results and improve performance.

Example: Caching with Redis

```
const redis = require('redis');
const client = redis.createClient();

async function getCachedUser(userId) {
  const cachedUser = await client.getAsync(userId);
  if (cachedUser) {
```

```
  return JSON.parse(cachedUser);
}

const user = await getUserFromDatabase(userId);
client.setex(userId, 3600, JSON.stringify(user)); // Cache for 1 hour
return user;
}
```

6.2 Optimize Database Queries

Use proper **indexes** in MongoDB to speed up frequent queries, and avoid full table scans. Use the **explain()** function to analyze query performance.

```
db.users.find({ email: 'john@example.com' }).explain('executionStats');
```

Appendix B: MongoDB Cheat Sheet for Efficient Querying and Indexing

Welcome to **Appendix B**, your go-to **MongoDB Cheat Sheet** for efficient querying and indexing! Think of this appendix as your **Swiss Army knife**, a compact, powerful tool that will help you wield MongoDB like a pro. Whether you're writing queries, optimizing performance, or creating indexes, this guide will save you time and headaches.

In this appendix, we'll cover:

1. Basic CRUD Operations

2. Querying with Filters and Projections

3. Aggregation Pipeline Basics

4. Indexing for Performance

5. Common Query Optimization Techniques

We'll also sprinkle in some **fun facts** along the way to make your MongoDB journey a bit more entertaining!

B.1 Basic CRUD Operations

Let's start with the fundamentals: **CRUD** (Create, Read, Update, Delete) operations in MongoDB. These are the building blocks of any application that interacts with a MongoDB database.

1.1 Inserting Documents

To create (insert) a new document into a collection, use insertOne() or insertMany().

Example: Inserting a Single Document

```
db.products.insertOne({
  name: 'Laptop',
  price: 999.99,
  category: 'Electronics',
  stock: 50
});
```

Example: Inserting Multiple Documents

```
db.products.insertMany([
  { name: 'Phone', price: 599.99, category: 'Electronics', stock: 100 },
  { name: 'Headphones', price: 199.99, category: 'Accessories', stock: 200 }
]);
```

MongoDB automatically generates an **_id** field for each document unless you provide one.

1.2 Reading Documents (Queries)

To read documents, use find() for retrieving multiple documents and findOne() for retrieving a single document.

Example: Finding All Documents

```
db.products.find();
```

Example: Finding with a Filter

```
db.products.find({ category: 'Electronics' });
```

This query returns all products where the **category** is **'Electronics'**.

1.3 Updating Documents

To update documents, use updateOne() or updateMany(). These methods allow you to update fields in documents based on a filter.

Example: Updating a Single Document

```
db.products.updateOne(
  { name: 'Laptop' },  // Filter
  { $set: { price: 899.99 } }  // Update
);
```

Here, the price of the product named "Laptop" is updated to **899.99**.

Example: Updating Multiple Documents

```
db.products.updateMany(
  { category: 'Electronics' },
  { $set: { stock: 0 } }  // Set stock to 0 for all electronics
```

);

This query updates all products in the **Electronics** category by setting their stock to **0**.

1.4 Deleting Documents

To delete documents, use deleteOne() or deleteMany().

Example: Deleting a Single Document

db.products.deleteOne({ name: 'Phone' });

Example: Deleting Multiple Documents

db.products.deleteMany({ stock: 0 });

This removes all products with zero stock.

B.2 Querying with Filters and Projections

MongoDB provides powerful query operators that allow you to filter, sort, and project (select) data in very specific ways.

2.1 Basic Query Operators

Equality

The simplest query operator is equality ({ field: value }).

db.products.find({ price: 999.99 });

Comparison Operators

MongoDB offers several comparison operators, such as **$gt** (greater than), **$lt** (less than), **$gte** (greater than or equal), and **$lte** (less than or equal).

Example: Finding Products Priced Over $500

db.products.find({ price: { $gt: 500 } });

This query returns all products where the price is greater than 500.

Example: Range Query

db.products.find({ price: { $gte: 500, $lte: 1000 } });

This query retrieves products with prices between $500 and $1000 (inclusive).

2.2 Logical Operators

You can combine multiple conditions using logical operators like **$and**, **$or**, and **$not**.

Example: Combining Queries with $or

```
db.products.find({
  $or: [
    { price: { $lt: 200 } },
    { stock: { $gt: 100 } }
  ]
});
```

This query returns products where either the price is less than 200 **or** the stock is greater than 100.

2.3 Projections

Projections let you control which fields are included in the query result. To project fields, use the second argument in find().

Example: Projecting Specific Fields

```
db.products.find({ category: 'Electronics' }, { name: 1, price: 1, _id: 0 });
```

This returns only the **name** and **price** fields (excluding **_id**) for products in the **Electronics** category.

B.3 Aggregation Pipeline Basics

The **aggregation framework** is MongoDB's most powerful feature for data processing. It allows you to transform and aggregate data using a sequence of stages (a pipeline).

3.1 $match Stage

The $match stage filters documents, similar to find(). It's typically the first stage in an aggregation pipeline.

Example: Match Products with Price Over $500

```
db.products.aggregate([
```

```
  { $match: { price: { $gt: 500 } } }
]);
```

3.2 $group Stage

The $group stage groups documents by a specified field and allows you to apply aggregate functions, like **$sum**, **$avg**, and **$count**.

Example: Group Products by Category

```
db.products.aggregate([
  { $group: { _id: '$category', totalStock: { $sum: '$stock' } } }
]);
```

This query returns the total stock for each product category.

3.3 $project Stage

The $project stage reshapes documents, allowing you to include or exclude fields.

Example: Project Only Name and Discounted Price

```
db.products.aggregate([
  {
   $project: {
    name: 1,
    discountedPrice: { $multiply: ['$price', 0.9] }
   }
  }
]);
```

This query returns each product's name and its price after applying a 10% discount.

B.4 Indexing for Performance

Indexes are crucial for optimising query performance. They allow MongoDB to search data more efficiently, avoiding full collection scans.

4.1 Creating Single-Field Indexes

A **single-field index** is created on a single field, such as email or createdAt.

Example: Indexing the email Field

db.users.createIndex({ email: 1 });

This creates an ascending index on the **email** field.

4.2 Creating Compound Indexes

A **compound index** is created on multiple fields, and it's useful when you query by multiple fields in a predictable order.

Example: Indexing price and category

db.products.createIndex({ price: 1, category: 1 });

This compound index speeds up queries that filter by both **price** and **category**.

4.3 Understanding Indexes with explain()

To analyze how efficiently MongoDB uses an index, use the explain() method.

Example: Explaining a Query

db.products.find({ price: { $gt: 500 } }).explain('executionStats');

The output shows whether the query used an index or performed a full collection scan. You'll want to avoid full scans as they degrade performance.

4.4 Covering Indexes

A **covering index** is an index that includes all the fields required to satisfy a query, meaning MongoDB doesn't need to look into the actual documents.

Example: Creating a Covering Index

db.products.createIndex({ price: 1, name: 1 });

Now, a query that fetches products by **price** and **name** can use this index to avoid accessing the full document.

B.5 Common Query Optimization Techniques

5.1 Avoid Full Collection Scans

Full collection scans occur when MongoDB has to check every document in a collection to find matches. Always use indexes for frequently queried fields.

Solution: Ensure that your queries use indexed fields.

// Add an index on the 'price' field to optimize this query

db.products.createIndex({ price: 1 });

5.2 Use Projections to Limit Data Transfer

Avoid fetching unnecessary data from the database by using projections to limit the fields returned in your queries.

Solution: Use projections in your queries.

db.products.find({ category: 'Electronics' }, { name: 1, price: 1, _id: 0

});

This query only retrieves the **name** and **price** fields, reducing the amount of data transferred.

5.3 Limit Results for Large Queries

When dealing with large datasets, use **limit()** to restrict the number of results returned, preventing the application from becoming overwhelmed.

Solution: Apply a limit to your query.

db.products.find().limit(10);

This query returns only the first 10 products.

Appendix C: Reference Guides for Popular Libraries and Frameworks (Express.js, Mongoose, Jest)

Welcome to **Appendix C**, where we dive into reference guides for some of the most popular libraries and frameworks in the Node.js ecosystem: **Express.js**, **Mongoose**, and **Jest**. These tools form the backbone of many Node.js applications, so mastering them will make you a more efficient and confident developer.

This appendix is like a cheat sheet, designed to give you quick access to the most important features and patterns in these libraries. We'll include **full code examples** and diagrams to help you understand how to use these tools effectively.

Here's what we'll cover:

- **Express.js**: A minimal and flexible web application framework for Node.js.

- **Mongoose**: An elegant MongoDB object modeling tool for Node.js.

- **Jest**: A delightful JavaScript testing framework with a focus on simplicity.

C.1 Express.js Guide

1.1 Setting Up Express.js

Express.js is one of the most popular frameworks for building web applications and APIs in Node.js. Let's start with a simple setup.

Installation

npm install express

Basic Express Server

```
const express = require('express');
const app = express();
const port = 3000;

app.get('/', (req, res) => {
  res.send('Hello, World!');
});
```

```
app.listen(port, () => {
  console.log(`Server running at http://localhost:${port}`);
});
```

When you run this code, your server will listen on port **3000** and respond with **"Hello, World!"** when you visit the root URL (/).

1.2 Routing in Express.js

Routing is how Express directs requests to different endpoints (URLs). The app object has methods corresponding to HTTP verbs, such as **get**, **post**, **put**, and **delete**.

Example: Defining Routes

```
app.get('/users', (req, res) => {
  res.send('List of users');
});

app.post('/users', (req, res) => {
  res.send('User created');
});

app.put('/users/:id', (req, res) => {
  res.send(`User with ID ${req.params.id} updated`);
});

app.delete('/users/:id', (req, res) => {
  res.send(`User with ID ${req.params.id} deleted`);
});
```

This example defines RESTful routes for managing users. The :id in the route is a route parameter that can be accessed using req.params.

1.3 Middleware in Express.js

Middleware functions are functions that have access to the **request**, **response**, and **next** objects. They are used to modify requests or responses, execute code, or terminate the request-response cycle.

Example: Using Middleware

```
const loggerMiddleware = (req, res, next) => {
  console.log(`${req.method} ${req.url}`);
  next(); // Move to the next middleware or route handler
};

app.use(loggerMiddleware);

app.get('/', (req, res) => {
  res.send('Hello, with logging!');
});
```

In this example, **loggerMiddleware** logs the method and URL of every request. The next() function tells Express to move on to the next middleware or route handler.

1.4 Handling JSON Requests

Express.js has built-in middleware to parse incoming JSON payloads. This is useful for handling JSON in API requests.

Example: JSON Request Handling

```
app.use(express.json());

app.post('/users', (req, res) => {
  const user = req.body;
  res.send(`User ${user.name} created!`);
});
```

In this example, **express.json()** parses incoming JSON requests, and the server responds with the name of the user sent in the request body.

1.5 Error Handling Middleware

Express provides a special type of middleware for handling errors. Error-handling middleware has four arguments: err, req, res, and next.

Example: Error Handling

```
const errorHandler = (err, req, res, next) => {
```

```
  console.error(err.stack);
  res.status(500).send('Something went wrong!');
};
```

```
app.use(errorHandler);
```

Any error thrown in the app is caught by this middleware, which sends a **500 Internal Server Error** response.

C.2 Mongoose Guide

2.1 Setting Up Mongoose

Mongoose is an **ODM (Object Data Modeling)** library for MongoDB and Node.js. It allows you to define schemas, interact with MongoDB, and perform data validation.

Installation

```
npm install mongoose
```

Connecting to MongoDB

```
const mongoose = require('mongoose');

mongoose.connect('mongodb://localhost:27017/myapp', {
  useNewUrlParser: true,
  useUnifiedTopology: true
}).then(() => {
  console.log('MongoDB connected');
}).catch(err => {
  console.error('MongoDB connection error:', err);
});
```

2.2 Defining a Schema and Model

Mongoose schemas define the structure of your documents in MongoDB, including field types, validation rules, and default values.

Example: User Schema and Model

```
const mongoose = require('mongoose');
const userSchema = new mongoose.Schema({
  name: { type: String, required: true },
  email: { type: String, required: true, unique: true },
  password: { type: String, required: true },
  createdAt: { type: Date, default: Date.now }
});

const User = mongoose.model('User', userSchema);

module.exports = User;
```

In this example, we define a **User** model with fields like **name**, **email**, and **password**. We specify that the **email** field must be unique and required.

2.3 Creating and Saving Documents

Once the model is defined, you can create and save documents using the model's methods.

Example: Creating a New User

```
const newUser = new User({
  name: 'John Doe',
  email: 'john@example.com',
  password: 'securepassword'
});

newUser.save()
  .then(user => console.log('User created:', user))
  .catch(err => console.error('Error creating user:', err));
```

2.4 Querying Documents

Mongoose models provide several methods to query the database, including find(), findOne(), findById(), and where().

Example: Querying for a User by Email

```
User.findOne({ email: 'john@example.com' })
  .then(user => console.log('User found:', user))
  .catch(err => console.error('Error finding user:', err));
```

2.5 Updating Documents

To update a document, you can use methods like updateOne(), updateMany(), or findByIdAndUpdate().

Example: Updating a User's Email

```
User.findByIdAndUpdate(userId, { email: 'newemail@example.com' }, { new:
true })
  .then(updatedUser => console.log('User updated:', updatedUser))
  .catch(err => console.error('Error updating user:', err));
```

In this example, the new: true option returns the updated document.

2.6 Deleting Documents

To delete a document, use deleteOne(), deleteMany(), or findByIdAndDelete().

Example: Deleting a User by ID

```
User.findByIdAndDelete(userId)
  .then(deletedUser => console.log('User deleted:', deletedUser))
  .catch(err => console.error('Error deleting user:', err));
```

C.3 Jest Guide

3.1 Setting Up Jest

Jest is a testing framework for JavaScript that provides a great developer experience with features like snapshots, mocks, and easy-to-read error messages.

Installation

```
npm install jest --save-dev
```

Add the following script to your package.json:

```
"scripts": {
```

```
"test": "jest"
}
```

3.2 Writing Your First Test

Tests are organised into **describe** blocks and **it** blocks. The **expect** function is used to make assertions.

Example: Basic Jest Test

```
// tests/sum.test.js
function sum(a, b) {
  return a + b;
}

describe('sum function', () => {
  it('should add two numbers correctly', () => {
    expect(sum(1, 2)).toBe(3);
  });
});
```

Run the test:

```
npm test
```

Jest will automatically find test files ending in .test.js or .spec.js.

3.3 Mocking Functions

Jest provides powerful mocking capabilities to simulate functions or modules in isolation.

Example: Mocking a Function

```
const emailService = {
  sendEmail: jest.fn().mockReturnValue(true)
};

describe('emailService', () => {
  it('should send an email', () => {
```

```
  const result = emailService.sendEmail('hello@example.com');
  expect(result).toBe(true);
  expect(emailService.sendEmail).toHaveBeenCalledWith('hello@example.com');
 });
});
```

3.4 Testing Asynchronous Code

You can test asynchronous

functions using **async/await** or **done** callbacks.

Example: Testing an Async Function

```
async function fetchData() {
  return new Promise((resolve) => {
   setTimeout(() => resolve('data'), 100);
  });
}

describe('fetchData', () => {
  it('should return data', async () => {
   const data = await fetchData();
   expect(data).toBe('data');
  });
});
```

Appendix D: Key Terms in Clean Architecture and Software Design

Think of this section as your translator for all those fancy terms thrown around in meetings, blog posts, and textbooks. By the end, you'll be dropping terms like "Dependency Inversion" and "Sagas" like a seasoned pro.

Grab a coffee, and let's get nerdy!

A

Abstraction

A technique for hiding complexity by exposing only the relevant details. In Clean Architecture, abstractions (such as interfaces) allow higher-level modules to depend on abstract definitions rather than concrete implementations, making systems more flexible.

Example: Instead of directly interacting with a MongoDB database, you interact with a UserRepository interface, which abstracts the details of how data is stored or retrieved.

```
//Abstracting database logic
class UserRepository {
  save(user) {
   /* Implementation hidden */
  }
  findById(userId) {
   /* Implementation hidden */
  }
```

Aggregation

In MongoDB, aggregation refers to the process of transforming or combining data using the Aggregation Framework. It is commonly used to perform operations like grouping, sorting, and calculating averages.

Example: Aggregating the total sales for each product category.

```
db.orders.aggregate([
```

```
  { $group: { _id: "$category", totalSales: { $sum:    "$price" } } }
]);
```

API (Application Programming Interface)

A set of rules and tools that allows different software components to communicate with each other. In Clean Architecture, APIs are part of the Presentation Layer, where users or other systems interact with the application.

B

Bounded Context

A concept from **Domain-Driven Design (DDD)** that defines clear boundaries within a system where specific terms, entities, and processes are relevant. Each bounded context has its own models and logic, reducing ambiguity and overlap between parts of a system.

Example: In an e-commerce app, Product may mean something different in the Inventory context than in the Order context.

C

Clean Architecture

A software design approach that emphasises separation of concerns by organising code into distinct layers. Each layer has a specific responsibility, and dependencies flow inward, ensuring that the core business logic (domain) is protected from external influences like databases or user interfaces.

Layers: **Domain**, **Application**, **Presentation**, **Infrastructure**.

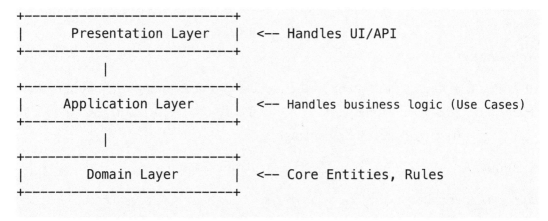

```
+-------------------------------+
|      Presentation Layer       |   <-- Handles UI/API
+-------------------------------+
            |
+-------------------------------+
|      Application Layer         |   <-- Handles business logic (Use Cases)
+-------------------------------+
            |
+-------------------------------+
|        Domain Layer            |   <-- Core Entities, Rules
+-------------------------------+
```

```
            |
+---------------------------+
|    Infrastructure Layer   |  <-- Databases, External APIs
+---------------------------+
```

Command Query Responsibility Segregation (CQRS)

A pattern that separates read operations (queries) from write operations (commands). This separation allows different models for reading and writing data, making systems more scalable and maintainable.

Example: A service might have separate methods for placing an order (write) and fetching all orders (read).

```
// Command (write)
placeOrder(orderData);

// Query (read)
getOrdersByUser(userId);
```

Coupling

The degree to which different parts of a system rely on each other. Tight coupling makes systems harder to maintain and test, while loose coupling promotes flexibility and modularity.

Example: Using an interface (or abstraction) to decouple a service from its database, so the service can be tested without depending on the actual database.

D

Dependency Injection (DI)

A design pattern that allows dependencies to be **injected** into a class rather than the class creating the dependencies itself. This makes code more flexible and testable.

Example: Instead of hardcoding a repository in a service, you inject it as a parameter.

```
class UserService {
 constructor(userRepository) {
  this.userRepository = userRepository;
```

```
  }

getUserById(id) {
  return this.userRepository.findById(id);
  }
}
```

Dependency Inversion Principle (DIP)

One of the SOLID principles that states **high-level modules** should not depend on low-level modules; both should depend on abstractions. This ensures flexibility and makes the system easier to extend or modify.

High-level module ---> Interface <--- Low-level module

E

Entity

An object that encapsulates the core business logic and rules of a system. Entities are part of the **Domain Layer** and represent objects with a unique identity.

Example: In an e-commerce app, a **Product** is an entity with properties like **name**, **price**, and **stock**.

```
class Product {
  constructor({ id, name, price, stock }) {
    this.id = id;
    this.name = name;
    this.price = price;
    this.stock = stock;
  }

  isOutOfStock() {
    return this.stock === 0;
  }
}
```

Event-Driven Architecture (EDA)

A design pattern where services or components communicate by emitting and responding to events. Events are asynchronous, allowing for loose coupling between services.

Example: When a user places an order, the **OrderPlaced** event is emitted, which triggers multiple downstream processes (e.g., payment processing, inventory updates).

I

Inversion of Control (IoC)

A design principle where the control of creating and managing dependencies is inverted and handled externally (e.g., via a DI container), rather than inside the class. This keeps classes focused on their core responsibility.

M

Middleware

In Express.js, middleware refers to functions that have access to the **request**, **response**, and **next** objects. Middleware functions can modify requests, responses, and perform tasks such as authentication, logging, and error handling.

```
app.use((req, res, next) => {
  console.log(`${req.method} ${req.url}`);
  next(); // Pass control to the next middleware
});
```

Microservices

A software architecture pattern where an application is broken down into smaller, independently deployable services. Each service is responsible for a specific piece of functionality and communicates with other services over a network.

Example: An e-commerce platform could have separate microservices for **Orders**, **Payments**, and **Shipping**.

O

Open/Closed Principle

One of the **SOLID principles** that states software entities (classes, modules, functions) should be **open for extension** but **closed for modification**. You should be able to add new functionality without modifying existing code.

P

Presentation Layer

The outermost layer in Clean Architecture, responsible for handling interactions with users (or external systems) through APIs, web interfaces, or mobile apps. It typically contains controllers, GraphQL resolvers, or views in an MVC architecture.

Example: In an API, the **Presentation Layer** would handle incoming HTTP requests and forward them to the appropriate **Use Case**.

R

Repository Pattern

A design pattern that abstracts the logic for interacting with a data source (e.g., a database). The **Repository** acts as an intermediary between the domain and the data source, making it easier to swap databases or change data access logic without affecting the rest of the system.

```
class UserRepository {

  findById(userId) { /* Retrieve user from the database */ }

  save(user) { /* Save user to the database */ }

}
```

S

Sagas

In event-driven systems, Sagas are long-running transactions that manage the coordination of multiple services or components. They ensure that if part of a process fails, compensating actions can be taken to roll back previous steps.

Example: When placing an order, the saga manages steps like **charge payment**, **update inventory**, and **initiate shipping**. If payment fails, the saga compensates by rolling back the inventory update.

SOLID

A set of five principles for writing clean, maintainable, and scalable object-oriented code:

- **Single Responsibility Principle (SRP)**: A class should have one and only one reason to change.

- **Open/Closed Principle**: Software entities should be open for extension but closed for modification.

- **Liskov Substitution Principle (LSP)**: Subtypes should be substitutable for their base types.

- **Interface Segregation Principle (ISP)**: Clients should not be forced to depend on interfaces they don't use.

- **Dependency Inversion Principle (DIP)**: High-level modules should not depend on low-level modules; both should depend on abstractions.

T

Test-Driven Development (TDD)

A development methodology where tests are written **before** writing the actual code. The cycle follows:

1. **Red**: Write a test that fails.

2. **Green**: Write the minimal amount of code to pass the test.

3. **Refactor**: Clean up the code while keeping the test green.

U

Use Case

In Clean Architecture, a **Use Case** defines the application-specific business logic. It describes what the application does when a certain action is performed, like registering a user, placing an order, or processing a payment.

```
class RegisterUserUseCase {
  constructor(userRepository) {
    this.userRepository = userRepository;
  }

  async execute(userData) {
    const user = new User(userData);
    return await this.userRepository.save(user);
  }
}
```

V

Value Object

A Value Object is an object that is defined by its properties rather than a unique identifier. Value objects are immutable and used to represent simple concepts like Address, Money, or Date Range.

Example: An Address value object might have fields like street, city, and zipCode, but it doesn't have a unique identifier (like an entity would).

```
class Address {
  constructor({ street, city, zipCode }) {
    this.street = street;
    this.city = city;
    this.zipCode = zipCode;
  }
}
```

Understanding these terms will help you better grasp the architecture decisions that shape your applications, and allow you to communicate more effectively. Whether you're diving into microservices or dependency inversion, remember: jargon isn't scary once you know what it means!

www.ingramcontent.com/pod-product-compliance
Lightning Source LLC
LaVergne TN
LVHW081527050326
832903LV00025B/1656